BANGKOK

GW00701538

BANGKOK

John Hoskin

Photography by PHOTOBANK

Hong Kong

Published by The Guidebook Company Limited,
3/F, 20 Hollywood Road, Hong Kong

Although the Publisher and the Author of this book have made every effort to ensure
the information was correct at the time of going to press, the Publisher and the Author do
not assume and hereby disclaim any liability to any party for any loss or damage
caused by errors, omissions, misleading information, or any potential travel disruption
due to labour or financial difficulty, whether such errors or omissions result from
negligence, accident or any other cause.

Grateful acknowledgement is made to the following authors and publishers
for permissions granted:

Alfred A Knopf Inc. for
*Video Night in Kathmandu
and Other Reports from the Not-So-Far East.* © Pico Iyer 1988

Jonathan Cape Ltd for
A Dragon Apparent by Norman Lewis, © 1951 Norman Lewis
Reprinted by kind permission of Rogers, Coleridge & White Literary Agency

Distribution in the United Kingdom, Ireland, Europe and certain Commonwealth countries
by Hodder and Stoughton, Mill Road, Dunton Green, Sevenoaks, Kent TN13 2YA

Editor: Richard Lair
Series Editor: Claire Banham
Illustrations Editor: Caroline Robertson
Map Artwork: Chaiyan Siripala and Pairoj Jeerabun
Cover Concept: Raquel Jaramillo and Aubrey Tse
Front Cover: Candy Hicks

Photography: PHOTOBANK (12–13, 15, 16, 21, 29, 32, 56–57, 59, 60,
61, 70, 71, 74, 78–79, 83, 84–85, 89, 93. 94–95, 114–115,
117, 118–119, 129, 142), John Everingham (138–139);
Michael Freeman (7, 53); Ian Lloyd (24); Zane Williams (17, 27, 90–91)

British Library Cataloguing in Publication Data has been applied for.

Production House: Twin Age Limited, Hong Kong
Printed in Hong Kong by Sing Cheong Printing Co. Ltd.

Contents

Life in Bangkok

Bangkok is a paradox. On the surface it is a burgeoning modern city of high-rise concrete blocks shooting up so quickly that the skyline has been constantly changing for the last several years. The building boom continues and a thrusting, up-to-the-minute Western facade has been reinforced by the appearance of tinselled department stores and American fast food outlets. At the same time, Bangkok is quintessentially Thai preserving the culture, the traditions and the national traits that have always distinguished the Thai people and their capital.

Located on a flat alluvial plain, Bangkok stands on the banks of the Chao Phraya River some 40 km. (25 miles) upstream from its outlet into the Gulf of Thailand. This, the nation's major waterway, was once the focal point of the city and from it a network of canals (*klongs*) spread out to serve as the capital's highways and byways, giving rise to the old soubriquet, 'Venice of the East.'

Today, most of the *klongs* have been filled in to make way for the motor car, yet the river still bustles with commuter ferries, water taxis and strings of barges travelling down from the provinces. However, despite the construction of three new deluxe hotels on the river banks - flanking the world-famous Oriental Hotel - modern Bangkok largely turns its back on the river.

It is an unprepossessing city on first sight. It sprawls monstrously, its traffic is notorious, it is hot and dusty and its lack of a definable downtown area is confusing. Disorientation and discomfort are common first impressions. Yet the city is full of wondrous sights and behind the facade it remains first and foremost Oriental; Western looks and styles are mere borrowings and adaptations, perhaps veiling the indigenous, but certainly not supplanting it.

It requires a little work to discover the charm of the place, but the effort is well rewarded. Once captivated by Bangkok's spell, the visitor is well and truly entranced. The Thai capital really does have a subtle power of enchantment, a power which is not dependent solely on physical attributes.

In his study of Bangkok, author Alec Waugh expressed most succinctly what it is that makes the city tick, that gives it unique appeal. 'Bangkok has been loved,' he wrote, 'because it is an expression of the Thais themselves, of their lightheartedness, their love of beauty, their reverence for tradition, their sense of freedom, their extravagance, their devotion to their creed - to characteristics that are constant and continuing in themselves.'

It is precisely the lively sometimes contrasting mix of national traits – adaptability mixed with conservatism, love of classical beauty alongside a weakness for the gaudy, joy in the moment and respect for the past – that makes Bangkok a vibrant blend of old and new which can confuse the first-time visitor. Balancing it all is the constant nature of what might be termed 'Thai-ness'.

Fundamental to continuity in Thai life since the founding of the nation have been Buddhism and the monarchy. Both these interwoven threads in the social fabric are highly visible in Bangkok.

The everyday impact of the national religion can be readily seen in the early morning as files of monks make their daily alms rounds, the same as has been happening for centuries. The backdrop of towering buildings and impatient commuter traffic only adds wonder to the timeless scene, while the city itself draws definition from it.

In a rather more fabulous fashion, Buddhism enlivens the city with the amazing architecture of its many temples – some 400 of them. In the soaring, glazed-tiled roofs and gilded spires of Bangkok's historic *wats* the visitor glimpses a picture of medieval Oriental splendour, the very stuff of Eastern fairytales. Wat Phra Keo (Temple of the Emerald Buddha), Wat Arun (Temple of the Dawn) and Wat Po (Temple of the Reclining Buddha), to name but three, are masterpieces in their own right, and contained within them are treasures of religious art that typify Thailand's cultural endeavour.

Equally as important as Buddhism in maintaining national continuity is the monarchy and a tradition of regal guidance and grandeur which is still very much a part of Bangkok. The monarchy is now constitutional rather than absolute (as it was until 1932), but the King remains as deeply loved and respected by the people as ever, and royal anniversaries are a matter of great public celebration - witness the crowds at the Pramane Ground on the night of the King's birthday in December.

Moreover, much of the ancient royal ceremonial survives to make up a significant slice of city life. The most obvious example of this is the annual Ploughing Ceremony, a rite held in May for blessing the rice planting season presided over by the King and conducted with great pomp and majesty.

Bangkok is indeed the very heart of the nation, not just in the modern sense of being the focus of political and economic activity, but in a traditionally symbolic way too. Embodying the idea of the city as fountainhead of the nation is the presence of the Emerald Buddha, Thailand's most revered image, which is enshrined in Wat Phra Keo at the Grand Palace. The fate of the statue has always been linked with the security of the country as a whole, and the boundless honour in which it is held is illustrated in the thrice-yearly ceremony of changing its seasonal attire, a sacred rite that may be performed only by the King.

Further evidence of Bangkok's symbolic role is seen at the Lak Muang ('city foundation pillar'), abode of the city's guardian spirits. The pillar's shrine, standing opposite Wat Phra Keo, daily receives a flock of devotees who come to make offerings and pray for divine assistance.

The full import of the symbolism of Bangkok and the essence of tradition is to some extent lost on the foreigner because he persists in calling the place Bangkok. Meaning the 'Village of the Wild Plum', Bangkok was the name of the tiny trading settlement on the east bank of the Chao Phraya River before capital city status was conferred. To the Thais it is always Krungthep, 'City of Angels', these being just the first words in a glorious string of titles which the Guinness Book of World Records lists as the world's longest place name.

The full name in Thai reads: *Krungthep Mahanakhon Bovorn Rattanakosin Mahintharayutthaya Mahadilokpop Noparatratchathani Burirom Udomratchaniveymahasathan Amornpiman Avatarnsathit Sakkathattiya-avisnukarmprasit.* This translates as: Great City of Angels, the Supreme Repository of Divine Jewels, the Great Land Unconquerable, the Grand and Prominent Realm, the Royal and Delightful Capital City Full of Nine Noble Gems, the Highest Royal Dwelling and Grand Palace, the Divine Shelter and Living Place of the Reincarnated Spirits.

Despite the religious, royal and symbolic significance of Bangkok, it is true that the physical appearance of the city has suffered through the stresses and strains of latter-day economic development. Virtually all moves towards industrialization and the creation of a modern business infrastructure have been concentrated on the capital. A certain beauty, order and symmetry has thus been sacrificed to 20th century needs and the pursuit of material affluence.

However, what is perhaps more remarkable than the staggering growth of recent decades is the amount of the city's historical heritage which has been preserved. There are few monumental sights in Bangkok but there is much, often tucked away, that is quietly magnificent. The city seduces by a gentle unfolding of surprise rather than by any obvious vaunting of charms . . . so you must look in order to see.

To give but one example, the Grand Palace is justifiably at the top of everyone's sightseeing list, but before rushing to see the treasures within, slow down and savour the approach. After turning the corner of uninspiring Rajadamnoen Avenue you are confronted by a panorama of sweeping green and orange roofs, of gold spires and coloured brilliance framed by white crenellated walls below and a deep blue sky above. It is a stunning skyline, as spectacular a cityscape as you'll find anywhere.

Similar surprises, albeit usually on a smaller scale, are scattered throughout the city. There are, of course, the 'musts' - the major temples, the National Museum and so on - but there are plenty of other sights tucked away, their fascination increased by their unexpected discovery.

An instance here is the Erawan Shrine, a statue to the god Brahma that is popularly held to be an infallible source of good fortune. Thronged by devotees and classical dancers, swamped by flower garlands, incense and other offerings, it is an archetypal Oriental image -

yet there it stands right on the corner of one of Bangkok's busiest traffic intersections. It is an arresting sight and should you chance by on a bus you will notice that perhaps half the passengers (and maybe, alarmingly, the driver too) will raise their hands in a *wai* to the shrine.

As you begin to explore the city it reveals itself not as a monstrous and uniform urban labyrinth but as a place diverse in moods and looks. The area around the Grand Palace, the original heart of Bangkok, is classical Thai while the new royal district in Dusit (where Chitralada Palace, the present residence of the Royal Family is located) is a pleasant blend of East and West. Here wide tree-lined avenues, the Italianate old National Assembly and the Marble Temple display Thai looks incorporating certain European influences that were in vogue at the turn of the century.

Chinatown, with its cramped streets and clutters of shops and stalls, projects an air of frenzied commercial activity vastly different from the sedate and modern business and shopping districts centred on Silom and Surawong roads.

Tram in Chinatown, 1910

Everyday Religious Objects

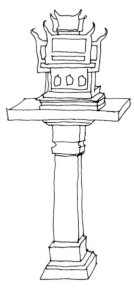

Amulets — Thais have great faith in the power and efficacy of amulets and most will wear at least one (some have half a dozen or more) on a neck chain. Commonly contained in a gold case with a clear plastic front, these amulets are usually tiny Buddha images which have been blessed, though less commonly they can be likenesses of famous monks. Some charms are considered to bring general good fortune and well being, while others are held to have specific powers such as offering protection from bullets or knives. Hence some people will wear a whole chainful, each amulet giving the wearer its own special strength.

Spirit Houses — In the garden or compound of virtually every house, business premises, government office and public building there is a spirit house. Usually raised on a short column, these highly ornate miniature dwellings, in the form of little temples or old Thai-style houses, are provided as homes for the spirits who inhabit that particular plot of land. The belief is that while humans have taken over use of the site, the spirits must still have their own dwelling so that they do not become angered and thus bring misfortune. Much ceremony surrounds the positioning of a spirit house and once erected it must be constantly cared for with food offerings, flower garlands and so on in order that the spirits remain contented.

Puang-Ma-Lai — This is a small flower garland made of jasmine, the loop usually decorated with an orchid tassel. It is used as a kind of general purpose offering, favoured because of its sweet smell, and is placed over Buddha images, on spirit houses and so forth.

Sai Sin — Worn like a bracelet around the wrist, the *sai sin* is a thin piece of cotton cord which has been blessed by a monk and is believed to give protection against evil spirits. A *sai sin* is also placed by monks around the interior of a house or office during the ceremony to bless a new building.

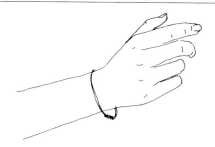

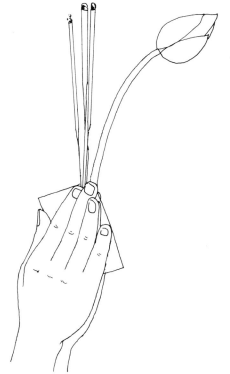

Temple Offerings — When praying at the temple Thais place three objects of offering in front of the presiding Buddha image — a candle, a lotus flower and incense. The candle symbolizes the light of understanding, and the lotus is considered an exalted flower, special to the Buddha (it is featured in many legends about the Enlightened One). For the incense there must be three sticks, which represent the Buddhist Triple Gem, standing for the Buddha, his teachings (the *dharma*), and the monkhood (the *sangha*).

Gold Leaf — Sold in little booklets, tiny squares of wafer-thin gold leaf are traditionally pressed on to Buddha images. In part this is done because Thais feel it is appropriate that the image is thus richly adorned, though there is a certain belief attached to the practice. If a person places gold leaf on a Buddha statue, it is believed he or she will receive certain benefit. There are three especially important places to put the gold leaf: on the mouth so that the giver will be blessed with good speech or sweet talk; on the head so as to become more wise; and on the chest over the heart to ensure a good heart in the sense of both health and kindness.

Diversity is very much a part of Bangkok's appeal and modern developments have their own kaleidoscopic attraction. An enormous variety of restaurants make the Thai capital one of Asia's most cosmopolitan spots for dining, while evening entertainment is almost legendary and has something to satisfy all tastes. Great choice of things to do and see is matched by an almost bizarre texture to the possibilities which range from cavernous discos to cosy jazz clubs, from skimpily-clad go-go dancers to agile Thai boxers, from visiting operatic performers to waitresses on rollerskates, from kung fu movies to classical Thai dance, and the list goes on.

During the day street scenes are equally diverting and kerbside life presents a wonderful *tableau vivant*. Noodle stalls rub shoulders with trays of imitation Rolex watches and Lacoste T-shirts, key-cutters, shoe repairers and a host of other tradesmen ply their business from pavement pitches, and amongst all the activity the throng of people is smiling and gay. Notice, too, that however poor a district might be the atmosphere is devoid of a sense of strife and the Thais, in both dress and manners, are neat and decorous.

Ultimately it is indeed from the people that Bangkok derives its unique flavour. The Thais are fun-loving, easy going and instinctively hospitable. Their propensity for *sanuk* (having a good time) is contagious and also serves to unite the disparate ingredients that make up the city.

In their exuberant way the Thais reach out for the contemporary, Western influenced delights. They relish the department store, the fast food outlet and all the other trappings of modernity, but they do not turn their backs on tried and trusted ways and values. Big Mac has arrived and is enjoyed - but the same old noodle vendor is likely still doing business on the street outside.

Above all else the people possess a tolerance that is rare and there is a very real sense of freedom about life in Bangkok. It may appear at times hectic, chaotic, frustrating, disorganized or even downright crazy, yet what finally affects you is the city's good natured acceptance of life with all its idiosyncrasies.

Overview

A tropical country lying approximately between latitudes 6° and 21° north, Thailand is located almost equidistant between India and China. Bordered by Burma on the west, Laos in the north, Kampuchea in the east and Malaysia to the south, it covers an area of 514,000 sq. km. (198,475 sq. miles) - about the size of, for example, France - and extends 1,650 km. (1,025 miles) on a north-south line and 800 km. (500 miles) east to west. The country's outline is extremely irregular, frequently likened to an elephant's head and trunk, and so practical distances are much less than maximum limits.

Thailand's population stands at 55 million (1989 estimate) with a growth rate of less than 2 percent per annum, down from more than 3 percent in the 1960s following the success of a nationwide family planning campaign. The majority of the people are ethnically Thai, though as the area has been something of a migratory crossroads, there is considerable ethnic diversity and Chinese, Mon, Khmer, Burmese, Malay, Lao, Persian and Indian strains are, to varying degrees, mixed with Thai Stock. Ethnic minorities – chiefly northern hilltribes, Lao, Vietnamese and Kampuchean refugees, as well as a number of South Asian Indian and other permanent foreign residents, account for about 6 percent of the total population.

Consequently there is a noticeable variation in physiognomy and physique among Thais, not just regionally but also locally. In one small village, for example, it is possible to see a wide range of skin tones. Taking districts as a whole, the inhabitants of the North display more Lao and Burmese traits; the South is influenced by Malays and in Bangkok roughly half the population has some Chinese blood.

Thailand remains basically an agrarian society and about three quarters of the population are connected with agriculture in some form or another. Virtually all major commercial, financial and industrial activity is concentrated in Bangkok, where more than one tenth of the population resides. Moves towards decentralization - the much heralded Eastern Seaboard Development, for example - are being made but for the time being the capital bears the greatest burden in sustaining national progress.

Consequently there is a marked difference between Bangkok and upcountry areas, and even the second city, Chiang Mai, is less than one-fortieth the size of Greater Bangkok.

Getting There

By air There are over 40 international airlines serving Bangkok's Don Muang International Airport, a regional gateway and one of Asia's busiest airports. Thai International, the national flag carrier, flies to

Bangkok from the US, Australia (Sydney, Melbourne, Brisbane and Perth), London, as well as a number of other major European, Middle Eastern and Asian cities.

Regionally, Bangkok is easily reached from Hong Kong (nearly 20 daily flights, various airlines), Beijing, Taipei, Manila, Singapore, Jakarta, Kuala Lumpur, Penang, Rangoon, Dhaka, Calcutta, and Kathmandu. Among the more exotic embarkation points are Kunming, in southwestern China, Hanoi and Vientiane.

By rail Comfortable and inexpensive express trains connect Bangkok with Penang, Malaysia (overnight) and Singapore (3 days and 3 nights, including an overnight stop in Penang).

Getting around Bangkok

Bangkok's streets can be quite intimidating to the first-time visitor with their Los Angeles-like sprawl, New York-style gridlock, Rome-style drivers and, to top it off, a haphazard confusion of streets and lanes, some of which seem to change name at every major intersection. There is, however, method hidden amidst the madness and, with a little practice, the intrepid traveller will quickly master the art of getting from A to B in Thailand's capital city.

Taxis For both the independent traveller and the tour-group member taking advantage of free time, taxis are the most oft-used means of conveyance in Bangkok. Taxi cabs are not equipped with meters. Instead, the fare is negotiated before getting in. (The exception to the bargaining rule is hotel taxis, whose fixed rates may be as much as two times the going 'street' rate.)

The fare depends on distance, your bargaining skills and time of day - rush hours add ฿10-20 to the fare. Expect to pay about ฿180 (฿300 for hotel taxi) to and from the airport. Once the fare is agreed upon, there should be no additions or surcharges; tipping is not customary.

Few taxi drivers speak English, so have your destination, as well as hotel name and address, written out in Thai.

Tuk-tuks A more direct encounter with Bangkok traffic can be had by flagging down one of the city's swarm of motorized trishaws, called *tuk-tuk* in Thai (presumably an onomatopoeic designation). Marginally cheaper than taxis, these insectiform buzz-bombs are popular with the locals for short hops and with tourists for joy-rides. *Tuk-tuk* drivers have a penchant for wild bursts of speed on the straightaways, and seem to draw sustenance from the exhaust pipes of smoke-belching buses idling at red lights; but try it once for the experience. Fares start at ฿10.

Buses Bangkok has an excellent and relatively easy-to-use city bus system. The fare for ordinary buses is ฿2 (no distance limitation); fares for air-conditioned buses range from ฿5-20, depending on the distance to your destination. Many of the air-conditioned bus routes cover quite a bit of the city - a comfortable and inexpensive way to take in the town.

River taxis Small passenger ferry boats or river taxis (*reua duan*) ply the Chao Phraya river, criss-crossing between various landing stages on both banks. It is a useful service for travelling from, say, the Oriental Hotel to the Grand Palace. Fares begin at 3 Baht and vary according to distance.

General Information for Travellers in Thailand

Visas

Visitors from most Western nations can obtain a 15-day, nonextendable transit visa upon arrival in Thailand. (This policy was being revised at the time of publication: check with the local Thai embassy or consulate to make sure your country is on the current "most-favoured nations" list.) For travellers anticipating a longer stay, tourist visas, valid for 60 days, should be obtained prior to departure. Application for a 30-day extension costs ฿500 (about US$18). Those planning to study or do business in Thailand must obtain a non-immigrant visa, valid for 90 days but generally not extendable. Note: there is a ฿100/day fine levied at the airport on those who overstay the

The omnipresent 'tuk-tuk'

term of their visa. All persons who stay in Thailand for a total of 90 days or longer in one calendar year must obtain a tax clearance certificate before leaving the country, whether or not they have earnings or income to declare.

Customs

Customs formalities tend to be rather cursory for Western tourists. Do not be daunted by the entry forms handed out upon arrival asking for the declaration of all watches, radios, etc. Personal effects in reasonable quantity need not be meticulously declared. Cash, travellers' checks and other monetary instruments with a cumulative value of more than US$10,000 must be declared, however.

No Thai cultural relics classified as antiques may be taken out of the country without a certificate from the Fine Arts Department. (This restriction does not apply to antiques originating elsewhere, such as Burma or China, purchased in Thailand.) In addition, no Buddha image, whether ancient or modern, may be exported. Travellers should also be warned that there are harsh penalties awaiting anyone caught smuggling illegal drugs and other contraband into or out of Thailand.

Health

There are no particular vaccination requirements, but inoculation against typhoid and tetanus is recommended, as is gammaglobulin, helpful in alleviating the symptoms of hepatitis A, which is endemic throughout Asia (avoid eating raw freshwater shellfish). Vaccination against cholera has proved to be largely ineffective, and is not recommended; consult your own doctor.

Parts of Thailand, particularly the mountainous areas in the north and the Laotian and Kampuchean border areas (including the Mekong River) are host to chloroquine-resistant strains of malaria. (There is no malaria in Bangkok or its immediate environs.) Fansidar, once widely prescribed as a preventative, has been found to cause severe allergic reactions in some people. Consult your own doctor.

Do not drink water from the tap anywhere in Thailand - bottled water and soft drinks are readily available throughout the country. Ice at roadside stands should be avoided, and care taken when eating seafood and raw vegetables outside of Bangkok. Most restaurants, however, both in Bangkok and upcountry, maintain reasonably high standards of hygiene, and undue caution need not inhibit one's enjoyment of Thailand's culinary offerings.

The most common minor maladies afflicting travellers to Thailand, as anywhere, are head colds, diarrhoea and constipation, for which the appropriate remedies should be brought along. In addition, visitors from the temperate zones should be particularly alert to the dangers of heat exhaustion and sunburn.

Health care in the major urban areas is excellent, and private hospitals in Bangkok are staffed mostly by Western-educated, English-speaking doctors.

Money

Currency The standard until of currency is the *Baht* (B), which is divided into 100 *Satang*. coins include 25- and 50-*Satang*, and the much more common 1-, 5-, and 10-Baht pieces. Bills come in 10, 20, 50, 100 and 500 Baht denominations.

Exchange Currencies and traveller's cheques can be exchanged at most (but not all) banks and hotels. Many banks have special foreign exchange windows which stay open evenings and weekends.

Credit cards Internationally recognized credit cards, such as Visa, Mastercard and American Express, are accepted at many of the more expensive hotels, restaurants and shops in Bangkok and at most first-class hotels in the smaller cities. Otherwise, cash is the primary means of exchange.

Tipping Outside of the major hotels and restaurants, tipping is not a common practice in Thailand. It is customary at restaurants, however, to leave the small change, generally from 5 to 20 Baht, for the servers.

Communications

Thailand's postal system is quite reliable for outgoing mail. Both local and long distance telephone systems are quite efficient; there is even direct-dial international calling available in some areas.

Telex and facsimile services are widely available - many hotels maintain business centres where these, and other services, such as copying, are available.

The most convenient way to send purchases home is to arrange for the shop to handle wrapping and mailing for your purchase. If you choose to mail your own parcels, it is best to go to Bangkok's main post office on New Road, which offers a packing service. Note that there is a 10 km. (22 lb.) limit on the weight of any one item sent through the mail.

Language In Bangkok, most hotel service staff, many shopkeepers, some waiters and waitresses and a few taxi drivers speak some English. Upcountry, English speakers are harder to come by, although in such popular tourist destinations as Chiang Mai, language is less of a problem.

The most widely used language in Thailand is, of course, Thai. Thai is a tonal, generally monosyllabic language, similar in many respects to Chinese (although the alphabet is derived from Devengari, an Indian script). Like Chinese, most Westerners find it very difficult to master, but learning a few useful phrases (See Thai Vocabulary, page 126) will come in handy and endear you greatly to your hosts.

Reading Material Bangkok boasts three English-language dailies, the *Bangkok Post, The Nation* and *The World*. In addition, the *International Herald Tribune* (printed in Singapore each morning) can be found in most hotel lobby bookstores and newsstands along with a wide selection of Western magazines and periodicals. In addition, there are a number of excellent English and other foreign-language bookstores in Bangkok, notably Asia Books on Sukhumvit Road between Sois 15 and 17.

Electrical Appliances Electric current is 220V a.c., 50 cycles. Both round and square plugs are used, so bring an adapter. Local AM and FM radio stations operate in the same frequency ranges as in the US and Europe.

Modern youth ('wai-run')

Climate Bangkok's climate can be divided into three seasons: warm and dry from mid-October to early March; hot from March to mid-May and rainy from mid-May to mid-October. The average annual temperature is 29°C (83°F), while the range is from 30°C (86°F) in the most uncomfortable month of April to 25°C (77°F) in December. The best time to visit is during December and January when it is pleasantly warm and skies are clear. Flooding can be a problem in Bangkok during the tail end of the rainy season, although prolonged rainfalls are rare. Note: in spite of the three seasons, most visitors from temperate climes find Bangkok hot and humid year round - a recent survey rated it the world's hottest metropolis in terms of annual average temperature.

Clothing Light cotton and linen clothing are best suited to Thailand's tropical climate. Thais dress informally, but neatly - the same will be expected of the visitor. Shorts, short skirts and other revealing outfits are suitable as beachwear only. Flip-flops should be likewise avoided, although sandals that cover the toes are acceptable daytime footwear. Since shoes are always removed before entering private homes and temple sanctuaries, a comfortable pair of slip-on oxfords or loafers is recommended. For jungle treks, bring along a pair of broken-in walking

Bangkok 7 ft (2 m) 13°45' N 100°28' E 37 years   **THAILAND**

	Temperature °F			Temperature °C			Relative humidity		Precipitation		
	Highest recorded	Average daily	Lowest recorded	Highest recorded	Average daily	Lowest recorded	0630 hours	1230 hours	Average monthly		Average no. days with 0.04 in + (1 mm +)
		max.	min.			max.	min.		%	%	in	mm	
J	100	89	68	55	38	32	20	13	91	53	0.3	8	1	J
F	106	91	72	56	41	33	22	13	92	55	0.8	20	1	F
M	104	93	75	62	40	34	24	17	92	56	1.4	36	3	M
A	106	95	77	67	41	35	25	19	90	58	2.3	58	3	A
M	106	93	77	71	41	34	25	22	91	64	7.8	198	9	M
J	100	91	76	70	38	33	24	21	90	67	6.3	160	10	J
J	101	90	76	71	38	32	24	22	91	66	6.3	160	13	J
A	99	90	76	72	37	32	24	22	92	66	6.9	175	13	A
S	98	89	76	69	37	32	24	21	94	70	12.0	305	15	S
O	100	88	75	64	38	31	24	18	93	70	8.1	206	14	O
N	99	87	72	56	37	31	22	13	92	65	2.6	66	5	N
D	100	87	68	52	38	31	20	11	91	56	0.2	5	1	D

shoes or sneakers. Don't forget to bring a hat and sunglasses - you'll need them, even in the 'rainy' season.

'Safari-style' dress shirt and pants for men, and mid- or full-length cotton dress, or skirt and blouse for women are the norm for evening wear - more elaborate attire, such as tie and jacket, is rarely necessary except at Bangkok's poshest hotel restaurants or at formal receptions. Laundry service at most hotels is fast and reliable. For same day delivery, clothes should be in by 8 a.m. - there is usually a surcharge for express service.

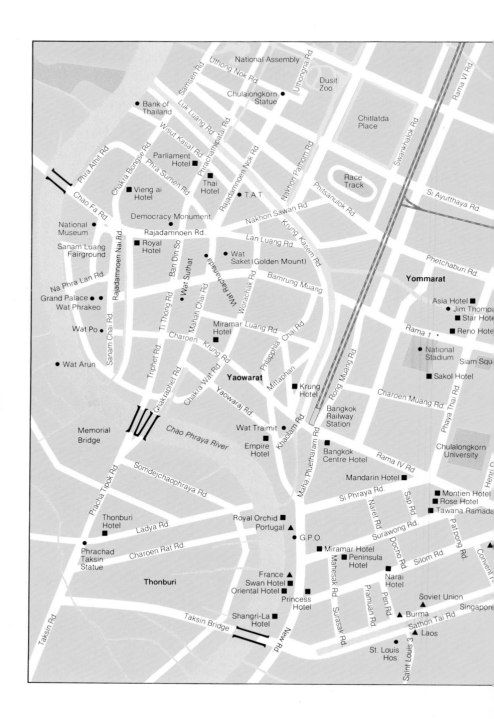

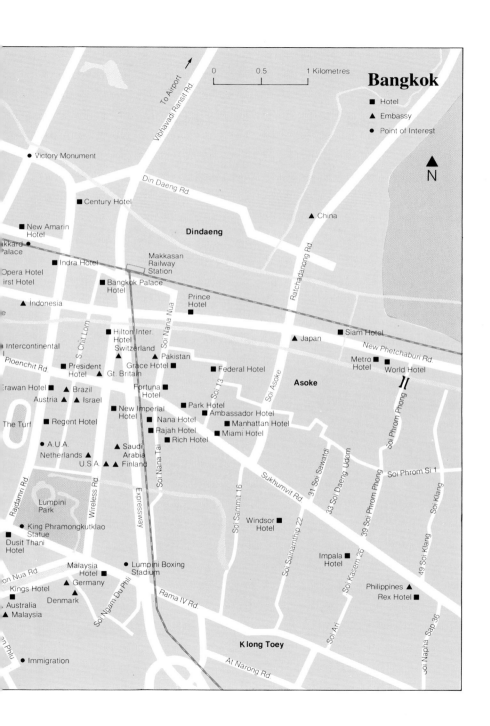

Bangkok

- ■ Hotel
- ▲ Embassy
- ● Point of Interest

N

To Airport
Vibhavadi Rangsit Rd

0   0.5   1 Kilometres

● Victory Monument

Din Daeng Rd

■ Century Hotel

▲ China

Dindaeng

■ New Amarin
Hotel

akkard ●
'alace

■ Indra Hotel

Opera Hotel

irst Hotel

■ Bangkok Palace
Hotel

Makkasan
Railway
Station

Prince
Hotel
■

Ratchadapong Rd

▲ Indonesia

e

Soi Nana Nua

S. Chit Lom

■ Hilton Inter.
Hotel
Switzerland ▲

▲ Pakistan

■ Japan

■ Siam Hotel

New Phetchaburi Rd

■ Intercontinental
l

Ploenchit Rd

■ President
Hotel ▲ Gt. Britain

Grace Hotel ■

■ Federal Hotel

Soi Asoke

Asoke

Metro ■
Hotel   ■
World Hotel

Soi Phrom Phong

rawan Hotel ■   ▲ Brazil
Austria ▲ ▲ Israel

Fortuna ■
Hotel

Soi 13

■ Park Hotel

The Turf   ■ Regent Hotel

■ New Imperial
Hotel

■ Ambassador Hotel

■ Nana Hotel   ■ Manhattan Hotel

■ Rajah Hotel   ■ Miami Hotel

■ Rich Hotel

● A.U.A.
Netherlands ▲
U.S.A. ▲

▲ Saudi
Arabia
▲ Finland

Soi Nana Tai

Soi Sawatdi

31 Soi Sawatdi

33 Soi Daeng Udom

39 Soi Phrom Phong

Soi Phrom Si 1

Soi Klang

Rajdamri Rd

Wireless Rd

Lumpini
Park

Expressway

● King Phramongkutklao
■ Statue
Dusit Thani
Hotel

Soi Sammit 16

Sukhumvit Rd

Soi Sainamthip 22

Windsor ■
Hotel

Soi Kasem 26

49 Soi Klang

on Nua Rd

Malaysia
Hotel ■

● Lumpini Boxing
Stadium

▲ Germany

Soi Ngam Du Phli

Rama IV Rd

Impala ■
Hotel

Soi Ari

Kings Hotel

Denmark

Philippines ▲
Rex Hotel ■

Australia

▲ Malaysia

n Phli

● Immigration

Klong Toey

At Narong Rd

Soi Napha Sap 36

Hotels

Bangkok offers an excellent choice of hotels in all categories and all price ranges. From "the Best in the World" (The Oriental according to a poll by US magazine *Institutional Investor*) down through every grade to budget guesthouses; from rates of over 2,000 Baht down to 50 Baht or less a night. There is something to suit all tastes and all pockets.

Except for the simplest guesthouses, hotels are airconditioned and have private bathrooms (shower rather than tub in the cheaper places). From the middle category on up, coffeeshops, restaurants, bars, nightclubs and swimming pools are standard facilities.

Following a recent building boom, Bangkok offers many deluxe class hotels that are comparable to the best in the world. Business services, fitness centres and superb speciality restaurants are found at all the top properties. You can also expect a high standard of service and many seasoned travellers rate Bangkok hotels as the best in Asia.

As the Thai capital has no readily definable downtown area, the choice between the best hotels is largely a matter of preferred location. You can go for a river frontage, a garden setting, a golf course or the closest approximation to the city centre.

The Dusit Thani Hotel overlooks exercisers in Lumpini Park

Listed below are some of Bangkok's leading hotels. Prices are for reference only and may change at any time. Luxury hotel bills are subject to a 10-25 percent tax and service surcharge.

Airport Hotel, 333 Chert Wudthakas Road, tel. 566-1020
Rates Baht 2,662 – 2,904 plus tax
300 rooms. Convenient for a one night stopover in Bangkok. Skybridge connects hotel to airport.

Ambassador Hotel, 8 Sukhumvit Road, Soi 11, tel. 255–0444
Rates Baht 1,400 – 2,800
Offers 935 rooms in three categories in three different wings: Chavalit wing (cheapest), Ambassador wing and the luxury Tower wing. Also noted for its 20 or so restaurants (European and Oriental specialities as well as fast food outlets) and Thailand's largest private collection of tropical birds. One of the best bargains in town.

Dusit Thani Hotel, Rama IV Road-Silom Road, tel. 233-1130, 233-1140.
Rates Baht 2,875 – 4,750
Long established as one of Bangkok's top deluxe hotels, the Dusit Thani has a high reputation for both accommodation (which includes its famous 'Landmark' guests rooms of 56 sq. m., the largest in Asia) and for dining offered in seven restaurants, each with its own culinary style. Good location in main commercial and entertainment district.

Hilton International, Nai Lert Park, 2 Wireless Road, tel. 253-0123
Rates Baht 3,000 – 5,700 plus tax
One of the city's finest luxury hotels with 343 rooms, the Hilton is further distinguished by its extensive landscaped tropical gardens, arguably the best in Bangkok. This is the place to stay if you are looking for a green and tranquil oasis, accessible but well away from the confusion and congestion of city streets.

Central Plaza Hotel, 1695 Phaholyothin Road, tel. 541-1234.
Rates Baht 2,700 – 3,400 plus tax
Located 15 km. from the city centre on the way to Don Muang international airport, this 607-room hotel has very extensive convention facilities and adjoins Bangkok's largest department store and shopping complex. Conveniently situated across the road is the 18-hole Railway Golf Course.

Imperial Hotel, Wireless Road, tel. 254-0111
Rates Baht 2,470 – 2,730
400 rooms. Tennis courts. Popular for conventioneers. Big discounts for
business people.

Landmark Hotel, 138 Sukhumvit Road (btw. Soi 4-6) tel. 254-0404, 0424
Rates Baht 3,000 – 3,400
　　Opened in 1988, the Landmark offers 415 rooms in its 31-floor
structure. An excellent penthouse restaurant (accessible by a glass outdoor
elevator that rises through an adjoining atrium shopping complex) offers
some of Bangkok's finest night viewing. The Landmark is sure to become a
mecca for Sukhumvit area shoppers and diners.

The Menam Hotel, 2074 New Road, Yannawa, tel. 289-0119, 289-0312
Rates Baht 2,400 – 2,800
727 rooms. On the river, also newly opened. Tennis courts, jogging
track. Suites up to Baht 22,000 per night.

Montien Hotel, 54 Surawong Road, tel. 234-8060/9
Rates Baht 2,200 – 3,500
The main advantage of this 485-room hotel is its location in the heart of
Bangkok's famous nightlife entertainment district.

Narai Hotel, 222 Silom Road, tel. 233-3350/89
Rates Baht 1,900 – 2,100 plus tax
500 rooms. Popular with Thais for its penthouse restaurant and lively
nightclub.

Oriental Hotel, 48 Oriental Avenue (off New Road), tel. 236-0400/9
Rates Baht 3,800 – 5,500 plus tax
One of Bangkok's oldest hotels (one small wing of the original late 19th
century building survives, but the main guest rooms are in two latter-day
wings), the 394-room Oriental is still considered by many travellers to be
Bangkok's finest and one of the best in the world. It is also Bangkok's
most expensive. Food and service are excellent as is the riverside
location.

The Regent of Bangkok, 155 Rajdamri Road, tel. 251-6244/6
Rates Baht 3,000 – 3,800.
Formerly the Peninsula Hotel, this 400-room property is superbly
designed and is well known for its lobby, a popular rendez-vous. Food
standard is also very high. The location is convenient (roughly midway
between the Sukhumvit and Silom districts) although uninspiring. One of
Bangkok's best shopping plazas is next door.

Rose Garden Hotel, 32 Petkasem Road, Nakhon Pathom, tel. 424-6850
Rates Baht 700-800
120 rooms. Golf, tennis, bowling, swimming, gardens, dancing, etc.
Located about 30 km. west of Bangkok.

Royal Orchid Sheraton, 2 Capt. Bush Lane, Siphaya Road, tel. 234-6860
Rates Baht 2,800 – 4,000
The 775-room hotel is on the banks of the Chao Phraya river but while
the view from the guest rooms is fine, the river frontage has not been
best utilized in the design of the public areas. Overall high standards of
comfort and food and beverage are maintained.

Shangri-La Hotel, 89 Soi Wat Suan Plu (off New Road), tel. 236-7777
Rates Baht 4,000 – 5,400
700 rooms. Enjoys a superb riverside location which rivals if not betters
that of the Oriental.
Exceptional views from the lobby.

Siam Inter-Continental, Rama I Road, tel. 253-0355/7
Rates Baht 2,800 – 3,400 plus tax
Well established and very popular, the 400-room hotel is one of
Bangkok's first top-ranked properties. Distinguishing features are its
fantastic architecture and extensive gardens with lake. Quiet and
pleasant.

Tawana Ramada Hotel, 80 Surawong Road, tel. 233-5710
Rates Baht 2,600 – 3,200 plus tax
265 rooms. Located on busy Surawong Street, Ramada took over
the Tawana from the Sheraton group.

Thai Food

The Thais are great eaters, not necessarily in quantity (they tend to eat a little frequently rather than a lot at once) but certainly in the way they relish their food. That essential trait *sanuk*, taking pleasure in life, finds full expression in dining, and Thais have a rare fondness for their national cuisine. For them other culinary arts simply do not compare.

Most visitors share this delight in Thai food and find it one of the world's truly great culinary treats, full of richness and variety. Yet pleasure in eating only partially accounts for the Thais' creativity in cooking. There is also the matter of ingredients and in this respect Thailand is most fortunate, with both the land and the surrounding sea yielding rich harvests. The staple, rice, grows in abundance as do the numerous varieties of vegetables, fruit, herbs and spices so beloved to the Thai palate. Pork and poultry are favoured meats, while many species of fish and crustaceans, both freshwater and from the sea, are popular and plentiful.

The basis of a Thai meal is, of course, rice. This is commonly steamed although it can be made into noodles, while glutinous or sticky rice is preferred with some speeialities. Accompanying are main dishes featuring vegetables, meat, seafood, egg and soup according to choice. Utensils are a fork and spoon and after helping yourself to a scoop of rice, you take small amounts from the other dishes as taste and appetite dictate. Like Chinese dining, it is something of a communal affair.

Besides the rice and other dishes, absolutely essential to any Thai meal are the sauces taken to give additional spice. For the novice there can be a bewildering number of these, but the most common are *nam plaa*, a liquid fish sauce which is extremely salty, and *nam prik*, also a liquid but with pieces of chillies, garlic, shrimp curd, sugar and lime. Care should be taken with the latter as the chillies can be very hot.

Although Thais generally prefer hot, spicy food, not all dishes are equally fiery. There are grades of hotness, some dishes being more spicy than others, and hence the sauces to add extra fire if desired. A word of warning, however; watch out for *prik-kee-noo*, tiny little green or red chillies which are hotter than hot. Provided these are treated with due caution, Thai food, while never bland, can be adjusted to suit most palates.

In the soup department, Thailand's great contribution to the culinary arts is *tom yam.*. This is a sour soup which can be made with various kinds of meat or fish but its most famous version is made with prawns: *tom yam goong*. The basic broth is flavoured with lemon grass, citrus leaves, lime juice, fish sauce and hot chillies.

Other common methods of Thai food preparation include curries, usually hot and spicy, and the stir-fried dishes which are cooked in a wok with pork fat oil, pepper and plenty of garlic. Then there is a wide choice of salad preparations (*yam*) made with just vegetables or with different kinds of meat or fish and mixed with distinctive flavourings such as lemon grass, fish sauce and such like, plus lime juice to give a characteristic sourness.

For dessert there are many sorts of local sweets *(kanoms)* often of a coconut flavour, and a vast array of tropical fruits, a minor gourmet discovery in themselves.

Below is a list of dishes which should provide a tasty introduction to some of the more common Thai specialities. It is only a very small sampling and the dedicated gourmet will find that one of the delights of Thai cuisine is that it offers almost endless possibilities of discovery.

Soup Apart from *tom yam goong* mentioned above, try *gaeng liang fak thong* (pumpkin and coconut); *gaeng jeud* (consomme with stuffed mushrooms - very easy on the palate); or *tom kah gai* (chicken cooked in coconut milk).

Seafood *Gaeng garee goong* (prawn curry); *goong phad phed* (fried prawns with chilli paste); *goong phad priow wan* (sweet and sour shrimps); *poo cha* (stuffed crab shells); *haw mok hoy* (steamed mussels); *plaa mueg phad phrik* (fried squid with hot sauce); *plaa khao laad phrik* (fried garoupa with chilli sauce); *gaeng kua pla* (fish and vegetable curry); *plaa phad khing* (fish with fresh ginger).

Poultry *Gai ob bai toey* (fried chicken in pandan leaves); *gaeng ped yang* (duck and vegetables); *gaeng phed gai* (curried chicken); *tom khem gai* (chicken casserole).

Rice and Noodles *Khao ob sapparod* (fried rice with pineapple); *khao phad phrik* (fried curried rice); *khao soi* (curried noodles).

Meat *Moo grawp* (crispy fried pork); *gaeng khiow wan* (green beef curry); *yam neua* (Thai beef salad); *phak look chin* (steamed pork balls with vegetables).

Vegetables *Gai phad khao phoot awn* (chicken with baby corn); *phak tom kati* (vegetables boiled with coconut milk); *phak dawng* (pickled vegetables).

Desserts *Sang-kaya gab khanoon* (coconut custard with jack fruit); *khao niow ma-muang* (sticky rice and mango).

Dining Out

Bangkok is a gourmet's (and gourmand's, for that matter) paradise and probably offers more restaurants to the square mile than any place in the world. And it is not simply the sheer number of establishments: there is also excellent quality (not necessarily expensive) and great variety with choices ranging from street stalls to posh grillrooms, and in styles of cuisine from Thai cooking to just about any national culinary offering. Below is a selective but by no means exhaustive list of restaurants; the adventurous diner will find plenty of scope to add to the list.

English

Bobby's Arms Pub and Restaurant
Patpong 2 Road Carpark Building
tel. 233-1759
Great fish and chips.

French

Le Vendome Restaurant
75/5 Soi II Sukhumvit Road
tel. 250-1220
Open 11:30 a.m.- 2:30 p.m.,
6:30 p.m.-11:00 p.m.
Closed Sunday lunch hours

German

By Otto
Btwn. Soi 12&14 Sukhumvit
tel. 252-6836
Open daily 9:00 a.m.-midnight
Bakery, beer garden, good food.

Scandinavian

Norden Restaurant
1 Soi 20 Sukhumvit
tel. 258-1496
Open daily 11:00 a.m.-11:00 p.m.
Smorgasboard Sun. noon-5:00 p.m.

Swiss

Fondue House
31/1 Wireless Road
(next to Swiss Embassy)
tel. 253-7559
Open daily 11:30 a.m.-2:00 p.m.,
6:00-11:00 p.m.
Features cheese and bourginogne fondues.

Lebanese

The Cedars
138 Sukhumvit Soi 49
tel. 392-7399
Open 6:30 p.m.-11:00 p.m. closed
Sundays
Order either the "Messe" or a main course, (fantastic lamb), the helpings are very generous!

Indian

Himali Cha-Cha
1229 New Road near the corner of
Surawong Road
tel. 235-1569
Open 11:00-11:00 p.m.
Fabulous chicken curries,
try the mango chutney.

Vietnamese

Le Dalat
51 Soi 23 Sukhumvit Road
tel. 258-9298
11:00 a.m.-2:00 p.m.; 6:00-11:00
Fine southern Vietnamese cooking
in an elegant but cosy atmosphere.
Try the marinated spareribs.

Italian

L'Opera
55 Soi 39 Sukhumvit
Open daily 6:00 p.m.-11:00 p.m.
Among the finest Italian food to be
found anywhere in Asia.
Proper dress please.

Japanese

Tokugawa Japanese Restaurant
Ambassador Hotel Complex
8 Soi 11 Sukhumvit tel. 251-5140
Open daily 11:00 a.m.-Midnight
The rather expensive but delicious
"Matsuzaka" beef is a speciality.

Korean

New Korea Restaurant
41/1 Sukhumvit Soi 19
tel. 253-5273
Open 8:00 a.m.-10:00 p.m.

Vegetarian

The Whole Earth Restaurant
93/3 Soi Langsuan, Ploenchit Road
tel. 252-5574
Open 4:00 -12:00 p.m.
Meat dishes also served.

Steaks

The Angus Steak House
9/4-5 Thaniya Road
tel. 234-3590
Open 11:30-11:00 p.m.

Chinese

New Great Shanghai Restaurant
648-652 Sukhumvit opposite Soi 35
tel. 258-7042, 258-8746
Open daily 11:00 a.m.-11:00 p.m.

The Golden Dragon
108-114 Sukhumvit Road,
near Soi 4
tel. 251-4553, 262-7412
11:00 a.m.-2:00 p.m. (Dim-Sum)
6:00 p.m.-10:00 p.m.

Thai

Ban Chiang
14 Soi Srivieng, off Silom Road
tel. 236-7045
Open 10:30 a.m.-2:30 p.m.,
4:30 p.m.-10:30 p.m.
Good food served in and about an
elegant Thai mansion.

Bussaracum
35 Soi Pipat 1 off Convent Road
Silom Road
tel. 235-8915
Open daily 4:00 p.m.-10:30 p.m.

Khrua Tao
Sukhumvit Soi 39
Open 11 a.m.-10:30 p.m.
Serves delicious seafood in a
convivial atmosphere.

Intimate
Ramkamhaeng Road
tel. 374-7175
Open 10 a.m.-11:30 p.m.
Gourmet Thai food served in a
cosy soft-lit atmosphere for
romantic dining.

Lemongrass Restaurant
5/1 Sukhumvit Soi 24
tel. 258-8637
Open 11:00 a.m.-2:00 p.m.
Delicious Thai 'nouvelle cuisine.'
Try the shrimps in orange sauce.

Piman Thai Theater Restaurant
46 Soi 49 Sukhumvit Road
tel. 258-7866
Open 7:00 p.m-9:30 p.m.
Reservations required.
Thai classical dance and music in a
traditional Thai setting.

Puang Kaew
Soi Prasanmitr,
off Sukhumvit Soi 33
tel. 258-3663
Open 10:30 a.m.-11:00 p.m.
Very popular with Thai gourmets.
Try the prawns in milk sauce.

Saem San Restaurant
65 Sukhumvit Soi 31
tel. 258-4582
11:00 a.m.-2:00 p.m.; 5:00-11:00
Oysters on the half shell, baked
crab claws and grilled Thai-style
steak are specialties here.

Sea Food Market
Sukhumvit Soi 16
tel. 236-0218
Open 11:45 a.m.-Midnight
A 'supermarket' restaurant where
you pick your own seafood to be
cooked to your taste.

Tumpnakthai Garden Restaurant
Rajadapisek Road
tel. 277-8833
Open 11:00 a.m.-11 p.m.
Seating over 3,000, this giant
garden restaurant still serves fine
food.
Waiters wear roller skates!

The Toll Gate
245/2 Soi 31 Sukhumvit Road
tel.258-4634
Open every day except Sunday
11:00 a.m.-2:00 p.m., 6:00-9:30
p.m.
Features 'Royal' cuisine.
Some of the best food in town, a
bit expensive but well worth it.

Yokyor Restaurant
4 Visukasut Road
tel. 281-1829
Open 11 a.m.-11 p.m. daily
Located on the Chao Phraya River
on board a converted river boat.

Useful Addresses

Telephone Information:

Local directory assistance
tel. 13
Domestic long distance
information
tel. 101
International directory assistance
tel. 100

Police (Special Tourist Branch)
tel. 281-0372, 281-5051, 199

Ambulance
tel. 281-1544, 199

Fire
tel. 281-6666, 281-1544, 199

Central Post Office
New Road
tel. 233-1050

Immigration
Soi Suan Plu
South Sathorn Road
tel. 286-7013/4, 286-7003

Railway Station (Hualamphong)
tel. 223-7461

International Airport Information
tel. 286-0190, 523-6201
Domestic Airport
tel. 281-1109, 281-1204

American Express Office
4th Floor Siam Center
965 Rama I Road
tel. 25104862/9

Bus Stations:
Eastern Bus Terminal
tel. 391-3301
North/Northeastern Bus Terminal
tel. 279-4484/7
Southern Bus Terminal
tel. 411-4978/9

Hospitals

Bamrungrad Medical Center
33 Soi Nananua (3) Sukhumvit
tel. 253-0250/933
emergency 251-0415

Saint Louis Hospital
215 Sathorn Tai Road
tel. 211-2769, 211-2053

Samitivej Hospital
133 Soi Klang (49) Sukhumvit
tel. 392-0011

Bangkok Adventist Hospital
430 Phitsanulok Road
tel. 281-1422, 282-1100

Churches

Assumption Cathedral
(Roman Catholic)
23 Oriental Avenue
tel. 234-8556

Holy Redeemer Church
(Roman Catholic)
123/19 Soi Ruam Rudee
tel. 252-5097

Calvary Baptist Church
Soi 2 Sukhumvit Road
tel. 25108278

Christ Church (Anglican/Episcopal)
Convent Road
tel. 234-3634

Banks

Bank of Thailand
Bangkhunprom
tel. 282-3322

Bangkok Bank
333 Silom Road
tel. 234-3333

Bank of America
2/2 Witthayu Road
tel. 251-6333, 251-6367

Chartered Bank
Saladaeng Circle, Rama IV Road
tel. 234-0821

Chase Manhattan Bank
965 Rama I Road, Siam Center
tel. 252-1141

Hongkong & Shanghai Banking
Corporation
64 Silom Road
tel. 233-5996

Department Stores

Central Department Store
306 Silom Road
tel. 233-6930/9

Sogo Department Store
Amarin Plaza, Ploenchit Road
tel. 252-9810/29

Robinson Department Store
2 Silom Road
tel. 235-6690

Rental Car Agencies

Avis Car Rental
981 Silom Road
tel. 233-0397

Royal Car Rental
2/7 Soi 20 Sukhumvit
tel. 258-1411, 258-1428

**Tourist Authority of Thailand
(T.A.T.)**

Bangkok (Head Office)
Ratchadamnoen Nok Avenue
tel. 282-1143/5

Pattaya
382/1 Chaihaad Road, Moo 10,
Banglamoong
tel. 418-750, 419-113
(Area Code 038)

Embassies

Australia
37 Sathorn Tai Road
tel. 286-0411

Burma
132 Sathorn Nua Road
tel. 233-2237

Canada
11th Floor Boonmitr Building
138 Silom Road
tel. 234-1561/8

China
57 Ratchadaphisek Road
tel. 245-7032, 245-7037/8

France
Customs House Lane
tel. 234-0950

Germany
9 Sathorn Tai Road
tel. 286-4227

India
4-6 Soi Prasanmit, Sukhumvit Road
tel. 258-0300/6

Indonesia
600-602 Phetchaburi Road
tel. 252-3135/40

Italy
92 Sathorn Nua Road
tel. 286-4844

Japan
1674 New Phetchaburi Road
tel. 252-6151/9

Malaysia
35 Sathorn Tai Road
tel. 286-1390/2

Nepal
189 Sukhumvit Road Soi 71
tel. 391-7240

Netherlands
106 Wireless Road
tel. 252-6103

New Zealand
93 Wireless Road
tel. 251-8165

Philippines
760 Sukhumvit Road
tel. 259-0140

Singapore
129 Sathorn Tai Road
tel. 286-2111, 286-1434

Sweden
11th Floor Boonmitr Building
87 Soi 5 Sukhumvit Road
tel. 234-3891

United Kingdom
Wireless Road and Ploenchit
tel. 252-7161/9

United States
95 Wireless Road
tel. 252-5040/9

USSR
1081 Sathorn Nua Road
tel. 234-9824

Airlines

Aeroflot Soviet Airlines
7 Silom Road
tel. 233-6965/7

Air France
3 Patpong Road
tel. 236-9279, 235-9280

Air India
Amarin Plaza, 16th Floor
Ploenchit Road
tel. 256-9147, 256-9614

Air Lanka
1 Patpong Road
tel. 236-9292/3, 236-0159

British Airways
2nd Floor Chan Isara Tower,
Rama IV Road
tel. 236-8655

Burma Airways
208 Surawong Road
tel. 234-9692

Cathay Pacific Airways
109 Surawong Road
tel. 235-6022/6, 233-6105

China Airways
Siam Center, Rama I Road
tel. 251-9656/9, 251-9750/2

Garuda
944/19 Rama IV Road
tel. 233-3873, 233-0981/2

C.A.A.C.
134/1-2 Rama IV Road
tel. 235-6510/1, 235-1880/2

Japan Airlines
1 Patpong Road
tel. 235-9105/18, 234-9113/18

KLM Royal Dutch Airlines
2 Patpong Road
tel. 235-5150/9

Korean Airlines
Dusit Thani Hotel, Rama IV Road
tel. 234-9283/9

Lufthansa German Airlines
331/1-3 Silom Road
tel. 234-1350/9

Malaysian Airlines System
98/102 Surawong Road
tel. 234-9790/4, 234-9795/9

Philippine Airlines
Surawong Road
tel. 233-2350/2

Qantas Airways
14-8 Patpong Road
tel. 236-0102

Royal Nepal Airlines
1/4 Convent Road
tel. 233-3921/4

SAS Scandinavian Airlines System
312 Rama I Road
tel. 253-5309

Singapore Airlines
2 Silom Road
tel. 236-0303

Swiss Air
1 Silom Road
tel. 233-2931

Thai International and Thai
Airways
89 Vibhavadi-Rangsit Road
tel. 234-3100, 280-0070/80

United Airlines
183 Rajadamri Road
tel. 253-0559

Shopping

Bangkok's department stores, shops and market stalls offer a wide array of interesting and beautiful items, with quite a few bargains to boot. Whether you are looking for a simple memento of your visit, or good opportunities for costly purchases such as fine quality sapphires and rubies for which Thailand is famed, you will find more than ample scope.

Shopping facilities have expanded enormously in the last few years with many new department stores and plazas springing up in different parts of the city. These are complemented by the growing number of deluxe hotels where quality shopping arcades are integral amenities. (Prices in the latter tend to be a little higher than elsewhere due to the more expensive rents the shops have to pay, though the arcades are convenient and do generally offer good standards.) Such modern developments coupled with established shops and traditional markets now make Bangkok one of the most attractive shopping centres in Southeast Asia.

Since the city has no clearly defined downtown area, shopping districts are spread out and there is no area of specialization. However, the three following sections of Bangkok can be recommended for the variety and quality of their shops: Silom-Surawong-New Road-Oriental Avenue (nearby the latter is the up-market Oriental Plaza which has a fine selection of quality buys, while just off New Road, next to the Royal Orchid Sheraton Hotel is the River City Shopping Complex); Rama I Road-Siam Square-Siam Centre (the longest established of the modern shopping areas); Rajdamri-Ploenchit-Gaysorn (this district has the largest concentration of department stores). There are also a number of traditional markets - the best for the tourist being the Weekend Market at Chatuchak Park - but these have been listed in the sightseeing section as they are interesting as much for strolling around as for dedicated bargain-hunting.

Most shops are open six days a week while several are also open on Sundays and public holidays. Opening hours are usually from 9.00 or 10.00 to 18.00 or 18.30, although many of the smaller establishments open earlier and close later in the evening.

With the exception of department stores and the largest shops, bargaining is not only practised but usually expected. With patience, a friendly smile and courteous determination you can expect discounts of 20-30 percent. Below are listed some general rules to follow when shopping in Bangkok's markets and shops:

•Touts are to be avoided. Such people are paid commissions by certain shops for introducing customers, and shoppers will rarely find a good bargain in this way.

•Receipts should be obtained for all purchases and, in the case of gems or antiques, you should ask for a certificate of authentication.

• As a simple safety precaution, it is advisable not to carry more cash than you expect to use that day. Make use of hotel safety deposit boxes.

• Major credit cards are accepted in the bigger establishments and shops specializing in the tourist trade.

• Many shops can package and ship purchases to your home address. If this is done, it is advisable to take out insurance coverage which the shop should be able to arrange.

Best buys for the intrepid shopper include:

Thai silk Handwoven and available in a wide variety of weights, colours and patterns, silk may be purchased either by length or as ready-made items of clothing.

Thai cotton Like silk, handwoven cotton is a traditional craft in rural areas. The cloth is ideal for both ladies' and men's clothing, and is especially suitable for Bangkok's hot, sticky climate.

Gems & Jewellery Bangkok is a major world centre for coloured gem stones which are both mined locally and imported for cutting. Best of the local stones are ruby and sapphire. Gems may be purchased either individually or as ready-made pieces of jewellery. Look for clear colour and good cutting as well as size. All good shops will give certificates of authentication.

Silverware Good price and high quality due to the skill of Thai silversmiths in both high and low relief work makes silver a good buy. Recommended items include bowls, cigarette boxes and the chunky silver jewellery produced by Thailand's northern hilltribes.

Nielloware Made of silver inlaid with black alloy, the craft dates back to the 17th century and the various products (from jewellery to cigarette boxes) are unusual and attractive.

Bronzeware Began virtually since the country was born with the casting of Buddha images, gongs and bowls. Popular buys include bronze cutlery sets, generally with rosewood handles.

Woodcarving An enormous range of items are carved out of solid teak. Animal figures (notably elephants), salad bowls, trays and so on are popular portable buys, while teakwood furniture is good and comparatively inexpensive. Most shops can arrange for the packaging and shipping of large items.

Lacquerware Items made from covering a bamboo frame with many layers of resin which, when dry, are painted and polished to a high gloss include boxes, chests, trays, small tables, and decorative plates. Colour schemes are black and gold, or orange, green and yellow.

Celadon pottery The art of ceramics flourished in Thailand during the Sukhothai period when King Ramkamhaeng settled Chinese potters in the country. The craft subsequently went into decline but has been revived in recent years. The distinctive high-fired green pottery is available in many forms; lamp bases, ashtrays, vases, figurines, etc.

Leathergoods Made from a variety of local skins (snake, crocodile and buffalo), leathergoods are becoming increasingly good value as the quality of finished goods improves. Shoes, handbags, wallets, belts, luggage and so on are all available.

Tailoring Bangkok is cheaper than either Hong Kong or Singapore for custom tailoring and, at its best, quality is as good.

Antiques Stone and bronze statues, woodcarving, Chinese porcelain, old jade, antique celadon, silver betel nut boxes, paintings from Thailand and other countries in Southeast Asia are among items to be found.

NOTE: there is a ban on exporting Thai antiques and even some *objets d'art* and non-Thai antiques require an export license. Details of any such formalities can be obtained from the shop owners. Also, faking antiques is a thriving industry. Some reproductions are very good and make worthwhile purchases provided they are priced as such and not as the genuine article. Also be aware that the export of Buddha images, old or new, is officially banned. It does not always work in practice, but you are advised to check with the Fine Arts Department (National Museum).

Khon masks Made from papier mâché and brightly painted to represent characters (especially demons and monkey warriors) from the *Ramakien* classic epic, these are used in the traditional Thai *khon* dance drama and make unusual and decorative souvenirs.

Paintings Classical paintings, both original and reproduction, decorative renderings of typical Thai landscapes and scenes, and modern works by leading contemporary Thai artists are available at a number of galleries to be found in Bangkok.

Thai Dolls These are popular souvenirs and are detailed and finely crafted models of classical Thai dancers, country folk and northern tribespeople in their various colourful costumes. Sold as both individual figures and tableaux with two or three characters.

Entertainment

Mention entertainment in relation to Bangkok and the idea most likely to spring to mind is a particularly licentious form of nightlife. Such is the city's reputation - famous or infamous depending on your point of view - that it is known for a nighttime scene largely orientated to the single male and pretty well unrivalled by anywhere else in quality and quantity. This reputation is not ill-founded. Bangkok does offer an unusually wide choice of nightclubs, go-go bars and massage parlours with an estimated 200,000-300,000 hostesses, bar girls and masseuses available to customers. In fact entertainment is not limited to the salacious and there is more choice than perhaps one would first think. Nevertheless, let's begin with the best known.

The main go-go bar areas are Patpong I and II, two small streets running between Silom and Surawong roads, and Soi Cowboy, a narrow lane between Sois 21 and 23 off Sukhumvit road. The former is the best known and for many the most exciting, although both districts are packed with bars. Some establishments are open in the afternoon but go-go dancing (usually several skimpily clad girls dancing at the same time on a small stage) officially gets underway at 6 p.m. and goes on until 1 or 2 a.m.. Customers drinks are around 40 Baht and the girls, when not dancing, are available for conversation, drinks (about the same price as customers' tipple) and invitations to go out. If a customer wishes to take out a bar girl before closing time there is a bar fine of 200-300 Baht; after hours it's simply an arrangement between two people.

Massage parlours (open 6 p.m. to midnight on weekdays and 2 p.m. to midnight on weekends and public holidays) are found throughout the city with concentrations in Patpong and New Petchaburi Road. As you enter you are confronted with a plate glass window (supposedly a one-way mirror but it rarely is) behind which sit scores of girls each with a number pinned to her dress. You make your choice, the attendant calls out the girl and off you go to a room (often quite luxurious) furnished with bed and bath. The procedure is for the girl to bathe you, then give a massage and whatever else you may be seeking. A variation on the normal massage is the body massage, or 'B-course', where the girl uses her entire body and not just her hands to massage; a lather of soap suds aids lubrication and makes it a most sensuous experience. Prices vary slightly from parlour to parlour but the average is around 160 Baht for a one-hour ordinary massage and 400-500 Baht for a one-and-a-half hours body massage. Payment for additional services is negotiable - reckon on at least 500 Baht.

Besides go-go bars and massage parlours there is a growing number of cocktail lounges, sometimes pretentiously termed 'executive lounges', where the formula is but a variation on an old theme. The places are bars, albeit of plusher decor than normal, with hostesses available for

An Old, Sad Song

*ven as they went about their very adult trade, the girls who worked
in the bars seemed little in more ways than the physical: hard and
easily hurt, they were just experienced enough to know how to
turn their innocence to advantage. Their sauciness was shy, their
bashfulness was brazen. One minute, they would stroke a foreigner's hand to gauge what kind of job he had; the next in order to
show him real affection. One minute, they were repeating endear-
ments imperfectly picked up from some American movie; the next,
forgetting themselves, they would admit to daydreaming about the
right man or a fairy-tale future.*

    *Inevitably, this elfin wish for happy endings rubbed constantly
against the details of the lives they led. Nearly every girl had a tale
to tell, and nearly always it was the same one. She grew up in a
village in a family of twelve. A local man came along when she was
in her early teens and promised to make her rich ('Thai men no
good'). He said she would make her fortune, but she ended up
making his. He said she would be 'a maid', then forced her to
become a slave. She bore him a child, she returned alone to her
village, she worked without joy or profit in the fields. Now she
could support her offspring only by coming to Bangkok. Who
looked after the child? 'Mamá.' Did her still devoted parents know
what she was doing in Bangkok? 'No. I tell them I work in
boutique. They know I work in bar, they kill me.' Sometimes there
were hazards in her job: a boss would force her to sleep with him,
or lock up the bar and screen blue movies. But she could always
find another opening, another show. In the countryside, she could
earn only $15 a month; here she took home thirty times as much,
leaving her more than enough to send $100 each month to her little
brother or her widowed mother.*

    *One day, she hoped, she could make enough money to return to
her village and raise her child (though, school-girl to the end, she
squandered her cash as soon as she got it on discos and flashy
clothes). And one day, she hoped, she would fly off to live with her
husband. After the wedding, he had been forced to return to
Australia, or California, or Holland. But he promised, he really
promised, to send her a visa. The plane ticket, he wrote, was in
the mail.*

Pico Iyer, Video Night in Kathmandu

conversation and drinks. There is no go-go dancing and entertainment is usually live music and occasionally fashion shows where the idea is to show off the girls rather than any clothes they may be wearing.

It should be pointed out that Bangkok's areas of more wild nightlife have little of the pathos or squalor normally associated with such places of entertainment; there is certainly nothing to compare with the gross nature of red-light districts in Western cities. In keeping with the Thai character, the idea of *sanuk*, having a good time, predominates, and whatever anyone (whether guest or employee) gets up to is his or her own business. Moreover, while nightlife attractions are primarily geared to the single male, it is not uncommon for female visitors to go to a bar or massage parlour, there are no restrictions.

Having said that, there is one little odd form of entertainment best suited to a small group of males: no-hands dining. This is an ordinary dinner (Thai or Chinese cuisine) with the difference that instead of you using a fork and spoon or whatever, a pretty young lady pops the food into your mouth for you, and so 'no-hands'. The best known no-hands restaurant is at the Galaxy entertainment complex on Rama I Road.

Moving on to more standard entertainment fare, movie theatres abound in Bangkok though the number of foreign films (with original soundtrack) is rather limited due to high import duties. Thai movies - there is quite a large local film industry - can be fun. They typically follow simple story lines in three basic modes - kung fu action, romance and slapstick comedy - and can usually be followed without understanding the dialogue. Movie theatre prices are inexpensive at around 20-50 Baht.

Alternatively, a number of bars around town screen first-run video movies with the original soundtrack. Here the show is free and you just pay for the drinks.

For something a little more cultural and ethnic, the National Theatre (near the Pramane Ground) has afternoon weekend performances of Thai classical dance drama. The same thing, abbreviated and rather less authentic, can be seen at the number of Thai restaurants which put on cultural shows to accompany dinner. Although very much geared for tourist consumption these can be most entertaining and colourful affairs.

Bangkok tends to be a hedonistic city and when it comes to the more conventional and highbrow kinds of entertainment - plays, concerts, ballet, opera and such like - there are no regular offerings. The city, however, is not a cultural desert and there are fairly frequent performances of classical music, theatre and ballet either by local troupes or by visiting artists.

The venues for such entertainment are varied and range from the National Theatre to university auditoria, major hotels and the various national cultural centres (e.g. the British Council, Alliance Francaise, AUA, Goethe Institute etc). To find out what is coming up in any one week check the entertainment pages of the Sunday editions of the two English language newspapers, *The Bangkok Post* and *The Nation*.

On the music scene most leading hotels have nightclubs and cocktail lounges where there is live musical entertainment in the evening. Performers are mainly Thai or Filipino and the standard can be good. For international singers the principal venue is the Tiara supper club at the Dusit Thani Hotel which has cabaret shows, sometimes by quite well known artists, changing roughly every 10 days or two weeks.

For sound with action, discotheques are extremely popular in Bangkok. Some are located in top hotels (Bubbles at the Dusit Thani, Diana's at the Oriental, and Hollywood at the Hyatt Central Plaza, for example) while others are independent affairs, the best known of these being the cavernous 'The Palace' on Vibhavadi Rangsit Road (on the way to the airport) and the recently opened NASA Superadome off Ramkhamhaeng Rd.. The difference between the two types is that the former tend to be rather more sedate and cater more to overseas visitors and older clientele; the latter kind are more wild and attract the young crowd.

Last but by no means least there is Thai boxing. This exciting spectator sport is unique to Thailand and deserves to be described at some length.

Thai Boxing

Thai boxing *(muay-thai)* is the national pastime of Thailand. At first glance it seems to be a rather violent and vulgar affair: a kind of streetfight in a boxing ring. The spectators, almost exclusively male, are loud, vociferous, and apparently as much aficionados of the art of gambling as of *muay-thai* itself. Yet, like much in Thai society, a closer, more careful look reveals layers of culture, tradition and even aesthetic beauty that make Thai boxing more than merely thrilling entertainment (which, of course, it is).

As you jostle your way up to the ticket window through the teeming multitude of fans and vendors, you begin to sense that level of excitement usually associated with a crucial football match or a pennant-clinching baseball game: yet tonight's event is likely no more crucial to the fans or combatants than last night's or last year's. What you feel is the unvarying intensity of the Thai fight fans' passion for their national sport.

After making your way in and finding a seat (2nd-class seats are the best for watching the action both in the ring and the stands; 3rd-class is for inveterate gamblers and anthropologists; ringside is for the rich and famous), note the orchestra, seated on a platform to one side of the ring. Composed of traditional Thai instruments, it is an integral part of the ritual to follow.

The first two fighters enter the arena, followed by their trainer and handlers. Like their Western counterparts, they are wearing robes, boxing shorts, and 12- or 16-ounce boxing gloves. But there is something else: they are barefoot; around the left (or both) biceps is worn a white or colored armband (the *khruang-rang*), often with an amulet tied or sewn in; and a strange-looking headband (the *mong-khon*), which is worn only during the pre-fight ritual. This has been bestowed upon the fighter by his teacher and is a hallowed talisman.

The orchestra begins playing at a slow, steady cadence as the boxers begin their "boxing dance" *(ram-muay)*. It starts with a show of respect to the teacher *(wai-khroo)*, kneeling and bowing three times, much as one does when paying respect to the Buddha at the wat (indeed, the Buddha is first and foremost a teacher). The dance that follows is a combination of religious ritual (driving away evil spirits) and intimidation. The *ram-muay* is very difficult to master, and a boxer's display of proficiency in the dance will earn a fighter not only murmurs of admiration from connoisseurs in the audience, but respect for his fighting skills from his opponent as well.

During the fight which follows you will see the combatants exchange vicious blows to head and body using feet, fists, knees, elbows, in fact with virtually every potential weapon of the body except the head (butting is prohibited, as in Western-style boxing). The tempo and intensity of the music rises and falls with the level of intensity in the ring. All this clamor and fury may seem light-years removed from the spirituality and aesthetics of the *ram-muay*. Yet the paradox is explained if we look at the history of the sport.

Like the Chinese, Okinawan and Japanese martial arts (such as kung-fu, karate and judo), *muay-thai* began as a combination of self-defense and hand-to-hand combat techniques practised by warriors for use in battle. Over time, these techniques were refined and formalized by martial arts masters, who strung the best movements together into a kind of stylized dance, thus preserving and systematizing their teaching. The *ram-muay* is just such a series of fighting movements, a link to both the spiritual and martial traditions of the ancient Thai. And while boxing is a decidedly professional occupation — every fight, no matter where or when, is a prize fight — the concentration and discipline needed to master the pain and fear could not be attained without the devotional and spiritual training represented by the *wai-khroo* and the *ram-muay*.

The best place to see a *muay-thai* match in Bangkok is Lumpini Stadium, on Rama IV Road. Matches are held Tuesdays, Fridays and Saturdays beginning at 6:00 P.M. Lumpini is a funky, old wooden structure, smaller and more intimate than the other, more modern "Grand Palace" of Thai boxing, Rajadamnoen Stadium (matches Mondays, Wednesdays and Thursdays at 6, Sundays at 5).

On the Waterfront

angkok, the modern seat of government of Siam, has (according to the best authorities) two hundred thousand floating dwellings and shops,—to each house an average of five souls,—making the population of the city about one million; of which number more than eighty thousand are Chinese, twenty thousand Birmese, fifteen thousand Arabs and Indians, and the remainder Siamese. These figures are from the latest census, which, however, must not be accepted as perfectly accurate.

The situation of the city is unique and picturesque. When Ayudia was "extinguished," and the capital established at Bangkok, the houses were at first built on the banks of the river. But so frequent were the invasions of cholera, that one of the kings happily commanded the people to build on the river itself, that they might have greater cleanliness and better ventilation. The result quickly proved the wisdom of the measure. The privilege of building on the banks is now confined to members of the royal family, the nobility, and residents of acknowledged influence, political or commercial.

At night the city is hung with thousands of covered lights, that illuminate the wide river from shore to shore. Lamps and lanterns of all imaginable shapes, colors, and sizes combine to form a fairy spectacle of enchanting brilliancy and beauty. The floating tenements and shops, the masts of vessels, the tall, fantastic pagodas and minarets, and, crowning all, the walls and towers of the Grand Palace, flash with countless charming tricks of light, and compose a scene of more than magic novelty and beauty. So oriental fancy and profusion deal with things of use, and make a wonder of a commonplace.

A double, and in some parts a triple, row of floating houses extends for miles along the banks of the river. These are wooden structures, tastefully designed and painted, raised on substantial rafts of bamboo linked together with chains, which, in turn, are made fast to great piles planted in the bed of the stream. The Meinam itself forms the main avenue, and the floating shops on either side constitute the great bazaar of the city, where all imaginable and unimaginable articles from India, China, Malacca, Birmah, Paris, Liverpool, and New York are displayed in stalls.

Naturally, boats and canoes are indispensable appendages to such houses; the nobility possess a fleet of them, and to every little water-cottage a canoe is tethered, for errands and visits. At all hours of the day and night processions of boats pass to and from the palace, and everywhere bustling traders and agents ply their dingy little craft, and proclaim their several callings in a Babel of cries.

Daily, at sunrise, a flotilla of canoes, filled with shaven men in yellow garments, visits every house along the banks. These are the priests gathering their various provender, the free gift of every inhabitant of the city. Twenty thousand of them are supported by the alms of the city of Bangkok alone.

At noon, all the clamor of the city is suddenly stilled, and perfect silence reigns. Men, women, and children are hushed in their afternoon nap. From the stifling heat of a tropical midday the still cattle seek shelter and repose under shady boughs, and even the crows cease their obstreperous clanging. The only sound that breaks the drowsy stillness of the hour is the rippling of the glaring river as it ebbs or flows under the steaming banks.

About three in the afternoon the sea-breeze sets in, bringing refreshment to the fevered, thirsty land, and reviving animal and vegetable life with its compassionate breath. Then once more the floating city awakes and stirs, and an animation rivalling that of the morning is prolonged far into the night,—the busy, gay, delightful night of Bangkok.

Anna Harriette Leonowens,
The English Governess at the Siamese Court *(1871)*

History of Bangkok

Bangkok was founded as the Thai capital in 1782 by King Rama I. Prior to that it had been little more than a customs post and a small settlement of Chinese traders. Previous first city status had belonged for 417 years to Ayutthaya and, when that city was destroyed by the Burmese in 1767, briefly to Thonburi on the opposite bank of the Chao Phraya River (today part of Greater Bangkok).

When Rama I mapped out his plans for the new capital, it was his intention to build a city that would reflect the lost glory of Ayutthaya and restore national pride. The former capital had been an island city and so Bangkok was to follow suit. As the site stands on a broad loop in the river, it required only the cutting of canals in concentric arcs on the east flank to bring the water all around.

The royal palace had traditionally been the physical and symbolic heart of the nation. Accordingly, the Chinese traders were moved away from prime real estate on the banks of the river and the Grand Palace, a city within a city, was raised in their place.

And so it went as the capital developed, with palaces and temples reflecting those of Ayutthaya in their scale and magnificence; canals and waterways served as the communication arteries, producing a riverine metropolis much like the former capital.

Bangkok continued to look to the model of Ayutthaya throughout the first three reigns of the Chakri dynasty, each monarch adding to and

embellishing the city until it was one of the biggest and finest in the East. It was a well-planned city and had a clear centre, the Grand Palace, from which the various living and working districts of the general population radiated.

A radical shift in emphasis came in the mid 19th century beginning with the reign of King Mongkut, Rama IV (1851-1868). He ceased to look to the models of the past and instead sought to modernise the nation (and for all practical purposes that meant Bangkok) by opening up Thailand to the outside world. In 1855 he signed the first major trade agreement with Britain and treaties with other European powers and with the US quickly followed. Thailand's horizons now began to broaden through foreign contact and a deliberate development programme influenced largely by Western patterns.

Perhaps the single most significant turning point for Bangkok came in 1857 when King Mongkut ordered the construction of the first roads capable of taking wheeled traffic. The first of these, New Road, was completed in 1862. The city never looked back.

That was just the beginning and the expansion has continued apace ever since as the capital has been the focal point for all of Thailand's major commercial, financial, industrial and administrative activity: since 1900 the metropolitan area has expanded from 115 sq. miles to more than 580 and the population has grown from an estimated 460,000 to six million.

Sukhumvit Road traffic jam

Inevitably, in meeting the demands of such phenomenal growth, the balance and symmetry of the city have been upset. Nearly all the canals have now been filled in to make way for motor vehicles and building development has been dictated more by pragmatic considerations than aesthetic concerns.

Prior to World War II, new building in the capital mostly enhanced the cityscape, albeit following colonial rather than pure Thai design (for example, the headquarters of the East Asiatic Company next to the Oriental Hotel). But in the 1950s and '60s expansion was so rapid that practical demands outweighed all else. Hence the eminently functional and incredibly ugly shophouse, rows of three to four storey concrete retail outlets *cum* residences of unrelieved monotony.

It was not just the building which altered the appearance of Bangkok and disguised much of its original beauty. As the city expanded so did the focal point shift and gradually, with little or inadequate planning, any kind of downtown centre was lost in the haphazard sprawl.

In the light of Bangkok's rapid growth, it is not so much the modern veneer that is surprising, but rather the number of monuments of the past that have survived. Despite appearances the capital is as Thai as ever; it has, in typical fashion, merely adapted to changing circumstance. The historic sights may be partly veiled yet they manage to coexist with the latter day manifestations of this vibrant and exuberant city.

Sights of Bangkok

The Old Royal City

Topping any sightseeing list is the **Grand Palace** and **Wat Phra Keo** (Temple of the Emerald Buddha). These can be combined with other nearby sights integral to Bangkok's history and cultural heritage.

You can simply take a taxi to the Grand Palace, but to start off your sightseeing in style and sense the original mood of the old city, it is better to arrive by boat. The easiest way to do this is to take the Chao Phraya river taxi from the pier next to the Oriental Hotel (Oriental Avenue, off New Road) up to the Tha Tien landing stage by Wat Po, directly south of the Palace. Along the way you'll gain an impression of riverine life and the waterway that was once the capital's main artery.

Wat Po (Open daily) This is Bangkok's oldest and largest temple-monastery complex, and spans both sides of Chetupon Road with the temple compound on the left (with your back to the river) and the monks' quarters on the right. More correctly named Wat Phra Chetupon and popularly referred to as the Temple of the Reclining Buddha, Wat Po occupies the site of a 16th century temple, although it was radically

remodelled and enlarged in 1789 by King Rama I. Additions and restorations were also made in succeeding reigns.

Besides its size and age, Wat Po is remarkable for the wealth of structures and objects packed into the compound - chapels, pavilions, *chedis*, Buddha images and a profusion of statuary. Much of the latter bears witness to the fact that the temple was once a storehouse of learning and, for example, some of the stone figures illustrate techniques of traditional massage. (Massage and herbal medicine are still taught here and you can have a good and inexpensive limb-twisting massage at the pavilion on the left a little way inside the main entrance).

At first sight the mass of buildings seems confusing but the layout is actually quite ordered. The *bot*, or main chapel, lies ahead and slightly to the right of the entrance. It is in the middle of a courtyard surrounded by cloisters containing row upon row of gilded seated Buddha images. There are four small *viharns* on each side of the gallery, and a *chedi* and chapel stand at each of the four corners.

To the left of the visitor's gateway as you enter are four large *chedis* commemorating the first four Chakri kings), numerous smaller *chedis*, an old manuscript library, a Chinese and a European-style pavilion.

In the far left-hand corner of the compound is the large *viharn* which enshrines the enormous Buddha image which gives the temple its popular name. This is Thailand's largest statue of the reclining Buddha (the Enlightened One passing from his world into Nirvana) and measures 45 m. (145 ft.) long and 15 m. (50 ft.) high. It is made of brick covered with plaster and gold leaf and is an impressive sight although, filling virtually the entire interior of the *viharn*, it is difficult to fully appreciate its proportions. Most significant are the soles of the feet which are intricately inlaid with the 108 auspicious signs of the Buddha.

Also worthy of note are the marble bas reliefs around the base of the main *bot* depicting scenes from the *Ramayana*. Rubbings of these (now taken from cement casts) are widely sold as souvenirs.

The giant statue of the Reclining Buddha is what attracts most visitors, but time should be allowed for viewing the numerous other Buddha images in the smaller *viharns*, many having been brought from Ayutthaya and elsewhere in Thailand to embellish Bangkok after it was founded as the capital.

Wat Arun (Open daily) Across the river from Wat Po in Thonburi is Wat Arun or the Temple of Dawn. It is distinguished by a 86 m. (282 ft.) high *prang* raised on a series of terraces and decorated with embedded pieces of multi-coloured porcelain which catch the rays of the morning sun, hence the popular name. There are four smaller corner *prangs* and, on the lower terrace, four pavilions each containing a Buddha image.

The original temple was designated by King Taksin as his royal chapel when Thonburi was the capital, and until Rama I moved his base across to Bangkok, it briefly housed the Emerald Buddha. However, the

Devotion

A s we strolled together across the polished entrance hall towards the door, my attention was suddenly taken by what appeared to be a large, old-fashioned and over-ornate birdcage suspended in an environment in which nothing was more than a year old. I stopped to examine it, and the prince said, 'Uncle lives there'.

Although slightly surprised, I thought I understood. 'You mean the house spirit?'

'Exactly. In this life he was our head servant. He played an important part in bringing up us children, and was much loved by us all. Uncle was quite ready to sacrifice himself for the good of the family.'

The prince had no hesitation in explaining how this had come about. When the building of a new royal house was finished, a bargain might be struck with a man of low caste. The deal was that he would agree to surrendering the remaining few years of the present existence in return for acceptance into the royal family in the next. He would be entitled to receive ritual offerings on a par with the ancestors. Almost without exception, such an arrangement was readily agreed to.

'How did uncle die?'

The prince answered enigmatically: 'He was interred under the threshold. Being still a child I was excluded from the ceremony, which was largely a religious one. Everyone was happy. Certainly uncle was.'

I took the risk. 'Would a western education have any effect at all on such beliefs?' I asked.

'That is a hard question', the Prince said, 'but I am inclined to the opinion that it would be slight. This appears to be more a matter of feeling than conscious belief. Education is an imperfect shield against custom and tradition.' We stood together in the doorway and the cage swayed a little in a gust of warm breeze. 'In some ways', the prince said, 'you may judge us still to be a little backward.' His laugh seemed apologetic. 'In others I hope you will agree that we move with the times.'

Norman Lewis, 'Siam'

principal buildings were renovated and the central prang vastly enlarged during the reigns of Rama II and Rama III.

The Grand Palace and Wat Phra Keo (Open daily 8:30, Admission to Wat Phra Keo 100 Baht) Directly north of Wat Po are the massive white battlements enclosing Wat Phra Keo and the buildings of the Grand Palace. The main entrance is on the north side (furthest from Wat Po) on Na Phralan Road.

Here is the perfect introduction to the whole matter of Thailand, the Buddhist faith, regal grandeur and a deep respect for tradition. Though no longer the royal residence, and used only on special state occasions, the Grand Palace nevertheless remains the symbolic heart of the capital. Moreover, Wat Phra Keo, occupying one corner of the extensive compound, enshrines the nation's most revered Buddha image and is still the principal royal chapel.

The earliest palace buildings date from 1782, the year Bangkok became the capital, while succeeding monarchs added extensively to the work begun by Rama I. In consequence the Palace presents an intriguing mix of architectural styles from pure Thai to Victorian and Italian Renaissance. The Grand Palace comprises five major buildings:

Chakri Maha Prasat lies directly ahead of the main gate, beyond the entrance to the inner courtyard. Built in the reign of Rama V and designed by a British architect, it has an Italianate facade topped by a triple-spired Thai roof. Such a contrasting mix of styles is surprisingly successful and the effect, if strange, is generally pleasing.

Dusit Maha Prasat to the right of Chakri Maha Prasat, was built by Rama I and is a particularly fine example of Thai architecture of the Rattanakosin period. Formerly an audience hall, it is now used for the lying-in-state of kings.

Ampon Phimok Pavilion next to Dusit Maha Prasat, is an exquisite structure raised to allow the King to transfer from his shoulder-high palanquin and enter the robing room where he donned the attire in which he gave audience in the adjacent Throne Hall.

Amarin Winitchai Hall stands to the left of Chakri Maha Prasat. Constructed in Thai style by Rama I, it was formerly the royal court of justice and is now used as the coronation room.

Borombiman Hall on the far left, a comparatively modern and uninspiring structure, was built to accommodate state visitors.

Wat Phra Keo Fascinating though these and the smaller buildings are, they are completely outshone by Wat Phra Keo, the most famous and most stunning of Bangkok's more than 400 temples. It occupies the northeast corner of the palace compound (to the left after the main entrance).

This royal chapel, built by Rama I to enshrine the Emerald Buddha, is not only the single most important Buddhist temple in the country, it is also the one sight visitors remember above all else. It is quintessential

Wat Phra Keo and the Grand Palace

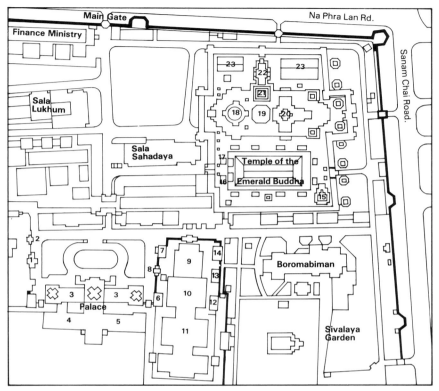

1. Royal Reception Hall
2. Ampon Phimok Prasat
3. Chakri Maha Prasat
4. Sumut-Devaraj-Ubbat Hall
5. Moonstarn-Baromasna Hall
6. Hor Phra Dhart Monthien
7. Dusida-Bhiromya Hall
8. Sanamchandr Hall
9. Amarin Winitchai Hall
10. Paisal-Taksin Hall
11. Chakrabardi Biman
12. Nor Phrasulalava Biman

13. Rajruedi Hall
14. Hor Satrakom
15. Hor Kantharasdr
16. Hor Rajbongsanusorn
17. Hor Rajkornmanusorn
18. Phra Sri Ratana Chedi
19. Phra Mondhob
20. Prasat Phra Debidorn
21. Model of Angkor Wat
22. Phra Viharn Yod
23. Hor Monthien Dharma
24. Hor Phra Naga

ⓣ Ticket booth

— — — Visitors entry and exit routes

Higher and Higher

According to the Laosian idea, the centre of the world is Mount Zinnalo (called in Siamese Mount Meru), which is half under water, and half above. The subaqueous part of the mount is a solid rock which has three root-like rocks protruding from the water into the air below. Round this mountain is coiled a large fish, called "Pla anun," of such leviathan dimensions that it can embrace and move the mountain: when it sleeps the earth is quiet, but when it moves it produces earthquakes.

Above the water is the inhabited earth, and on each of the four sides of Mount Zinnalo are seven hills rising in equal gradations one above the other, which are the first ascents the departed has to make. If he is wanting in "merit," he cannot get to the top; but, having got to the summit, he now comes to the different chambers in heaven.

The first heavenly space, immediately on the summit of Mount Zinnalo, is Tja to maha la chee ka taua, which is the abode of good spirits, and where also resides a king or chief called Phya Wett So'wan.

A step higher up is Tawah tingsah nang tewa nang, here live the persons who when on earth built Salas, and houses for the priests, and to each of them is allowed 16,000 wives. Phya In is the chief of the company here, and he receives his orders from above.

The next chamber of heaven is Tut sida tewa. The folks residing here are those who when on earth wore white clothing, and passed the time in saying prayers, and each of these pious individuals has 30,000 wives.

Chamber No. 4 is the Yama tewa, inhabited by both sexes, who when on earth performed works of great merit.

The fifth heaven is Nimma nalatee, also an abode for good persons. Each man has 60,000 wives.

Heaven No. 6 is Para min mitta, a home where the people have perfect peace; they spend their time in singing and dancing, and one hundred and five millions of wives are allotted to each gentleman.

Beyond this is a heaven divided into three chambers or kingdoms, each of which is subdivided again into three compartments as follows:—

A a. Poma tewa *is for both sexes, who have more merit than "Indra."*

A b. Maha pom ma, *also for men and women of the highest order; here reside the four regents of heaven.*

A c. Poma palo pitta, *likewise for people of both sexes, whose business is to take care of heaven.*

In B are the three places, or highest heavens, reserved for those who have made great merit to enjoy for a season "felicity" and "glory" before going to Nirwana—a is for gentlemen, b for priests, and c for ladies.

In C reside the three orders of angels:—

C a. Theweda newa sunja, *only for females.*

C b. Tewa butt utang, *for men only, who are the most perfect angels and reside here before becoming gods, and ruling over men, like Buddha.*

C c. *Those who have merit enough to attain this point become mothers of gods.*

Above all is Outer Darkness or "Nirwana," which Buddha is said to have compared to the disappearance of gunpowder when lighted in your hand. By some the word Nirwana is accordingly interpreted to mean "non-existence," but I doubt if this is the correct interpretation.

According to Mr. Alabaster, who is without a doubt the highest authority on Siamese Buddhism, it is "a place of comfort where there is no care: lovely is the glorious realm of Nirwana;" and I agree with Mr. Alabaster that it is a place of perfect happiness. On ancient figures of Buddha inscriptions are often found in which the maker of the image implores the aid of Buddha in reaching the "highest heaven." If the inferior heavinferior heavens are the places of enjoyment described above, there would be no object in praying for removal thence to a place of non-existence or unconsciousness.

Carl Bock, Temples and Elephants, *(1883)*

Thailand as every traveller imagines it - a dazzling, colourful Oriental wonder in its collection of pavilions, gilded *chedis, prangs* and statuary of strange mythological beings. The blue tiles of the main temple building and the overall splendour of so much rich, decorative detail is indicative of pure Thai religious architecture in which surface decoration is an integral part of the design.

Surprisingly, this lavish decoration does not detract from the religious atmosphere; rather it produces an air of mystery and serenity which adds to the overall effect.

The temple is surrounded by a cloister, the inside walls of which are decorated with murals depicting scenes from the *Ramayana*. These were first painted in the reign of Rama III, but have been restored several times since. In the process they have lost some of their aesthetic purity, though they are still impressive and indicative of the original compositions.

In a line from the entrance to the temple compound are the Phra Sri Ratana Chedi, the Phra Mondop or library and the Prasat Phra Thepbidon, or Royal Pantheon, containing statues of the Chakri kings (it is open only once a year, on April 6, Chakri Day). Next to the Phra Mondop is a model of Angkor Wat constructed at the time when Thailand held sovereignty over Kampuchea.

The statue of the Emerald Buddha is enshrined in the splendid sanctuary in the southern half of the compound (in front of the entrance). The 75 cm. (2.4 ft.) high image (made of green jasper, not emerald) is impressively raised on a tall, orange pedestal. Its three costumes are worn according to the three seasons and changed by the King at special ceremonies held at the commencement of the hot, rainy and cool seasons.

The origin of the statue is a matter of conjecture and legend. Its recorded history begins in 1434 when it was discovered in Chiang Rai after lightning had split open an old *chedi*. It was then covered in plaster and did not attract special attention until that cracked too, revealing the true material beneath.

On learning of the mysterious image, the King of Chiang Mai (whose realm included Chiang Rai) ordered it to be brought to his capital. The journey was unexpectedly protracted as the elephant carrying the sacred statue called a halt at Lampang. This was taken as an omen and the Emerald Buddha was allowed to reside in that town for 32 years before finally being enshrined at Wat Chedi Luang in Chiang Mai in 1468.

In 1552 a prince of Chiang Mai removed the statue and took it to Laos where it remained (first at Luang Prabang and later at Vientiane) until it was restored to Thailand by General Chakri (later Rama I) in 1778.

Lak Muang (Open daily) The pavilion enshrining the city pillar or foundation stone stands across the street from the northeast walls of the

Grand Palace (opposite Wat Phra Keo). Here, covered in gold leaf is the pillar-like *lingam* erected by Rama I as the symbolic foundation of Bangkok as the capital.

The city's guardian spirit is believed to reside here and the shrine is popularly held as a source of good fortune, receiving throngs of supplicants daily. Offerings of thanks are made when wishes are granted and often take the form of hiring classical dancers to perform. Thus Lak Muang is one of the best places in Bangkok to see traditional Thai dance in an authentic setting.

Pramane Ground Stretching north from the Grand Palace is the open oval space of the Pramane Ground, meaning royal cremation ground, also referred to as Sanam Luang (Royal Field). Throughout Bangkok's history it has served as the royal cremation site (last used as such in 1985), but more generally it is the venue for a number of annual celebrations (the Ploughing Ceremony in May, the public gathering on the King's birthday in December), and a recreation area, especially popular during kite-flying from February to April.

Wat Mahathat (Open daily) Situated on the west side of the Pramane Ground, between Silpakorn and Thammasat Universities, is Wat Mahathat or Temple of the Great Relic. It was built by the Second King (King of the Palace at the Front, a sort of deputy monarch, usually a brother of the King) in the reign of Rama I. Its main buildings comprise two chapels and a *mondop*, although the temple is most important as the national centre for monks of the Mahanikai sect. It is a highly respected hub of Buddhist learning as well as being an important meditation training centre.

Wat Saket and The Golden Mount (Open daily) Located on the corner of Mahachai Road near its junction with Rajadamnoen Avenue is Wat Saket and the 78 m. (256 ft.) high artificial hill known as the Golden Mount. Its construction was started by Rama III, who wished to reproduce a similar structure existing in Ayutthaya, but not completed until the reign of Rama V. On the top of the hill, reached by a winding flight of 318 steps, is a gilded *chedi* enshrining sacred relics of the Buddha. There are superb views of the old city area to be had from this vantage point.

At the base of the mount is Wat Saket, dating from the Rama I period and thus one of Bangkok's oldest temples. The *bot* contains murals depicting scenes from the *Ramakien* with registers of praying angels above. In another hall there is a large statue of the standing Buddha, brought from Sukhothai by Rama I.

Wat Saket is also famous for its annual temple fair in November, the largest of its kind in Bangkok, with food stalls, sideshows and other traditional forms of entertainment.

Wat Rachanada (Open daily) Situated on the opposite side of Mahachai Road from Wat Saket. In the first courtyard of this temple is

Bangkok's best known amulet market, a largish covered area packed with stalls selling charms which are widely believed to provide the wearer with various forms of protection. Many other religious objects are on sale as well and this is a fascinating place to browse around.

The temple itself, from the Rama III period, is untypical and comprises a *bot* and two *viharns*. The former's interior is decorated with mural paintings showing scenes of paradise and hell and groups of angels in various parts of the sky. The *viharn* on the left is interesting for its unusual design and the several Rattanakosin-style Buddha images it houses. Behind the main buildings is the curious structure of the Loha Prasat, a pavilion raised on a three-step pyramid and representing a legendary edifice mentioned in the Buddhist chronicles.

Wat Suthat (Open daily) Located on Bamrung Muang Road, a little way southwest of Wat Rachanada. Built in the first half of the 19th century, Wat Suthat is impressive for the size of its *bot* and *viharn* (the former is probably the tallest in Bangkok). The interiors are no less remarkable, with superb murals and fine collections of Buddha images, including the massive Phra Buddha Chakyamuni which originally came from Sukhothai and is a masterpiece of that period's sculpture.

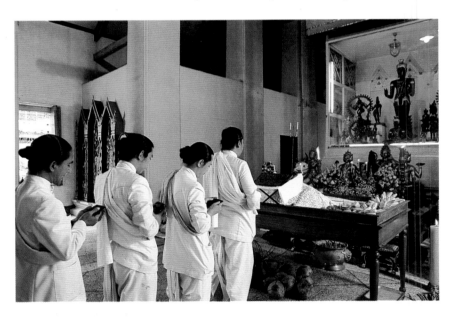

Brahman priests perform royal religious rites

Features of Temple Architecture

Thai temples are magnificent structures, impressive with their soaring multi-tiered roofs and stunning in their rich decorative detail. The *bot* (ordination hall) and *viharn* (hall for daily services), both similar in design, are the biggest and most important buildings, while the following architectural features and details should also be noted:

Chedi — A reliquary tower, synonymous with *stupa*. It is a solid monument, generally but not always tall and of massive proportions, enshrining relics of the Buddha, his disciples, or the ashes of important persons, religious or royal. There are various shapes of *chedis* but the most common is the bell-shape with a tall, tapering spire of graceful proportions. It can have a square base and sometimes, as in the Mon style of Haripunchai, have the form of a stepped pyramid.

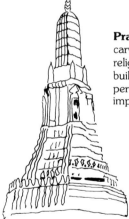

Prang — a tall, finger-like spire, usually richly carved. This was a common feature of Khmer religious architecture and was later adopted by Thai builders, typically in the Ayutthaya and Bangkok periods. In Thailand it appears only with the most important religious buildings.

Chofa — Translated as "sky tassel", this important architectural motif adorns the ridge-ends of the roof of a *bot* or *viharn*. It is a graceful finial in the shape of an elongated bird's head and neck and is commonly held to symbolize the *garuda*. A special ceremony at the conclusion of a temple's construction is held to raise the *chofa*.

Prasat — A tower sanctuary of Khmer origin. The word is sometimes used to refer to the collective structures of a Khmer temple. As adopted by Thai architects, the *prasat* is exclusively a royal or religious edifice, usually of a cruciform pattern and topped by a *prang*. The Golden Meru traditional royal funeral pyre, for example, is in the form of a *prasat*.

Sema — Symbolic foundation stones of a *bot* and the one feature which distinguishes that building from a *viharn*. Placed at the corner and axes on the outside of a *bot*, they are in the form of stone slabs, sometimes decorated with carving.

That — Another form of reliquary tower typically found in Laos and the northeast region of Thailand. It has a square base and a tall, tapering tower covered with decorative detail.

Mongkut — An architectural detail comprising tiers of discs rising in gradually diminishing size to a pointed finial. Used to top the *prasat* and other important religious buildings. The tiers represent the 33 levels of Buddhist perfection.

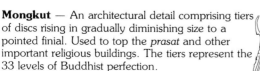

Giant Swing Opposite Wat Suthat are the towering twin poles of the *Sao Ching Cha*, or Giant Swing. Formerly this was the site of a Brahman festival to celebrate the god Siva's annual visit to earth. The highlight of the event involved teams of four young Brahmans, each of whom would swing through a 180 degree arc to a height of 25 m. (80 ft.) above the ground. The object of the exercise was for the man at the prow of the swing to try to grab between his teeth a bag of gold raised on a pole. It was a dangerous business and occasionally performers would fall to their death. The ceremony was officially abolished in 1935.

Wat Rajabophit and Wat Rajapradit (Open daily) These two temples lie southwest of Wat Suthat between Ban Mo and Sanam Chai Roads. Wat Rajabophit, constructed in 1863, is interesting for its stylistic originality, reflecting Rama V's fascination with Western art and architecture. The Italian Gothic interiors of the two chapels and the relief carvings of soldiers in European-type uniforms at the main entrance reflect these influences. A tall gilded *chedi* with four corner pavilions and a circular cloister distinguish the temples' layout. Rich ornamentation includes pieces of coloured porcelain and mother-of-pearl inlay on doors and windows.

A little way to the west across Klong Lot is Wat Rajapradit, another charming little temple rarely visited by tourists. The main building is raised on a stone platform and is covered in grey marble. There are open-sided corner pavilions and Khmer-style *prangs* on either side, while behind is a *chedi* built by Rama IV.

Wat Bovornivet (Open daily) Situated on Phra Sumen Road, about a block north of Democracy Monument, Wat Bovornivet is again slightly off the tourist map although well worth visiting. The buildings and their setting are interesting, but the temple is most important as the headquarters of the Thammayut monastic sect, which follows a stricter discipline than that of the traditional Mahanikai order.

Thammayut was founded by King Mongkut during his 27 years as a monk prior to his succession on the death of Rama III. Mongkut initially retired to Wat Mahathat and then later moved to Wat Bovornivet where he became abbot and founded the Thammayut order with a desire to return to the original purity of Buddhist teaching.

Because of this link with the dynasty, kings and royal princes have traditionally spent their time of monastic retreat at Wat Bovornivet.

The Dusit Area

What might be termed the new royal city lies to the northeast of Bangkok's historic heart in Dusit, an area largely developed by King Chulalongkorn, Rama V. Reflecting that monarch's fascination with Western styles, this district is characterised by comparatively wide, tree-lined streets.

The main approach is via the broad Rajadamnoen Nok Avenue which leads into the square in front of the old National Assembly, a building of Italianate design. It was constructed in 1907 as Chulalongkorn's Throne Hall. With the advent of the democratic system after the Revolution of 1932, it became the National Assembly until new premises were provided in 1974. The building is not normally open to the public.

In the centre of the square is an equestrian statue of King Chulalongkorn, while to the left are Amporn Gardens, an attractive park frequently the venue for royal-sponsored social functions and fairs.

Dusit Zoo (Open daily 8:00 a.m. to 6:00 p.m. Admission 10 Baht, children half price) Correctly named Khao Din (Mountain of Earth) Zoo because of the man-made hill which dominates the topography, this is one of the best zoos in Southeast Asia and is a popular spot for family outings. The park features a children's playground and lake with paddle boats in addition to the attraction of the animals.

Vimanmek Throne Hall (Open Wednesday-Friday 9:30 a.m. to 4:00 p.m. Admission 50Baht) Recently opened to the public as the private museum of Rama V, the four-storey wooden building behind the National Assembly opposite Dusit Zoo houses a collection of antique furniture, paintings and jewellery belonging to Thai Royalty.

East of Dusit Zoo is **Chitralada Royal Palace** which stands in extensive grounds and is mostly obscured from public gaze. It was constructed by Rama VI and adopted as the Royal residence by the present King.

Wat Benchamabopit (Open daily) This is the most famous sight in the Dusit area, located on Sri Ayutthaya Road between Chitralada Palace and the old National Assembly. Built by Rama V, it is the newest of Bangkok's royal temples and is a superb example of Thai religious architecture of the modern period. It is constructed largely from Carrara marble, hence the popular name 'Marble Temple'.

The *bot*, distinguished by its three-tiered roof of yellow Chinese tile and portico entrance with flanking statues of mythical lions, is an impressive sight, and the overall design of the temple, the work of Prince Naris, half brother to Chulalongkorn and accomplished man of the arts, is extremely pleasing.

Wat Benchamabopit is also famous for its courtyard gallery which houses more than 50 Buddha images (many are reproductions of

important statues) illustrating styles from all periods of Thai Buddhist art
and from other Buddhist countries. The presiding Buddha statue in the
bot is a copy of the highly revered Phra Buddha Chinaraj, the original of
which is at Wat Phra Sri Mahathat in Phitsanulok.

Chinatown

When Bangkok was designated as the capital, the Chinese traders
who had occupied the banks of the river were moved downstream to
make way for the Grand Palace. The resettled in the area known as
Sampeng, which is still the city's Chinatown. The district is close to the
southern curve of the Chao Phraya's broad loop and is traversed by
Charoen Krung (New) Road and Yaowaraj Road.

The area is characterized by narrow streets jam-packed with shops
and stalls offering an exotic mix of merchandise. The whole area is
pervaded by a frenetic air of commercial activity. Gold shops, always
painted red and white and making much use of mirror glass, are
Chinatown's most famous retailers, but you will also find many goods
that may be described as ethnic - traditional medicines made from tiger
bone, snake wine and other ingredients unheard of in the Western
pharmacopoeia; colourful paper models of houses, cars, refrigerators and
other symbols of material success which are burnt at funerals to ensure
the deceased every comfort in the hereafter. All this merchandise and
more is found piled high amid a jumble of buildings crammed into
seemingly impossible spaces thronged by hordes of buyers and sellers.

Chinatown is the sort of place to get lost in happily, wandering
where fancy takes you and seeing whatever there is to be seen. The
most typical of the district's streets, however, is Sampeng Lane (Soi
Wanit). This long, narrow pedestrian way is packed with all sorts of
stalls while at its northern end is Pahurat Cloth Market, popularly called
the Indian Market, with a contrasting mix of ethnic goods, notably
fabrics.

Also in Chinatown between Charoen Krung and Yaowaraj roads is
Thieves Market, more correctly called Nakhon Kasem. No longer the
'fence's' showcase that gave rise to its popular name, the market offers a
mix of modern goods and antiques cum *objets d'art*. Brassware is
abundant and other good buys include gongs, chests, cabinets and other
old furniture, Chinese porcelain and snuff bottles. Bargaining is *de
rigueur.*

There are a few Chinese temples tucked away in Chinatown, the
most important of which is **Wat Leng Noi Yi** on Charoen Krung. At one
time Bangkok's leading Chinese temple, it has a fascinating collection of
statuesand images, of various Chinese deities and of the Buddha, while
in the compound are workshops turning out paper funeral offerings.

At the southern end of Charoen Krung and Yaowaraj Roads,

near Hualampong Railway Station, just before Chinatown begins, is **Wat Traimit**, Temple of the Golden Buddha. Its attraction is its 3 m. (10 ft.) high solid golden statue of the Buddha which was rediscovered some 40 years ago when what was apparently a stucco Buddha was being removed from a ruined temple. The statue fell from the crane lifting it and the plaster cracked revealing the precious metal beneath. Fashioned in the Sukhothai style, it was probably coated with stucco to hide it from the Burmese when they invaded Ayutthaya in the 18th century.

Modern Bangkok

The districts in the southern and eastern parts of the city, referred to by their main thoroughfares, Silom and Sukhumvit respectively, comprise what might be termed modern Bangkok. Here and close by are to be found most of the major tourist hotels, along with the principal shopping, entertainment and commercial centres. Points of interest include:

Old Farang Quarter The stretch of Charoen Krung (New Road) at the river end of Silom Road is the site of Bangkok's old European quarter which blossomed in the late 19th and early 20th centuries. Reminders of this period are to be found in the Oriental Hotel (still the city's best and retaining one small original wing); the colonial style offices of the East Asiatic Company, doyen of the early foreign trading concerns; Oriental Plaza, again a colonial style building now converted as an up-market shopping centre; Assumption Cathedral, Bangkok's principal Catholic church; the French and Portuguese embassies and, next to the Royal Orchid Sheraton Hotel, the modern River City Shopping Complex.

A little further south on New Road, between the Silom and Sathorn intersections, is **Bangrak Market**, one of Bangkok's main fresh produce outlets. It is a traditional covered market, its outside thronged by cut-flower sellers (very cheap orchids).

Lumpini Park facing Rama IV Road opposite the Silom intersection, is the city's principal patch of greenery. The park has a lake with small paddle boats for hire. It is also the place to come early in the morning to jog or watch people practising Tai Ji Quan (Tai Chi), the ancient Chinese system of exercise and self-defence carried out in a kind of slow motion, shadow-boxing action.

Snake Farm (Open daily 8:30 a.m. to 4 p.m. Admission 10 Baht) Also on Rama IV Road near Lumpini Park is the Snake Farm at the Pasteur Institute which produces antidote for snake bites. It houses a large collection of cobras and other venomous snakes, which are *milked* daily at 11 a.m.

Erawan Shrine (Open daily) On the way towards the Sukhumvit area, on the corner of Ploenchit and Rajdamri Roads, by the side of the

Erawan Hotel, is the Erawan Shrine. Here a small but ornate pavilion enshrines a statue of Brahma, the four-headed Hindu god. It was originally constructed during the building of the hotel to ward off bad luck, but now it has become Bangkok's most famous source of good fortune, the deity popularly believed to be generous in the granting of all manner of wishes. The tiny area is packed daily with supplicants making wishes or giving traditional offering of thanks - flower garlands, incense, food, wooden model elephants (the elephant Erawan is the mythical mount of Brahma). Classical dancers also perform here. A curious and fascinating sight made more startling by its location at one of Bangkok's busiest traffic intersections.

Museums, Gardens

In addition to such places already mentioned, the following are worthwhile visiting:

National Museum (Open daily except Monday and Friday, 9 a.m.-12 noon and 1-4 p.m. Admission 20 Baht, free on Sunday) Located opposite the northwest corner of the Pramane Ground, the National Museum is the ideal complement to a tour of the old city. One of the largest and most comprehensive museums in Southeast Asia, it houses a fine collection of Thai sculpture from all periods, along with ethnological exhibits and examples of the performing arts, most notably marionettes and shadow theatre.

It offers, however, something more than just a collection of historic artifacts as it occupies part of the old Palace of the Front (built in 1782) and thus boasts a number of buildings that can be considered exhibits in their own right. Finest among these is the Buddhaisawan Chapel, one of the best examples of monastic architecture of the early Bangkok period. Constructed in 1787 to house the greatly revered Buddha image of Phra Buddhasihing, its walls are decorated with excellent murals depicting scenes from the life of the Buddha.

Other buildings of note in the museum compound include the residential quarters of King Pin Klao, Second King of Rama IV; the Isarawinitchai Hall, formerly the audience hall of the Palace of the Front; the Manghalaphisak pavilion, and the Tamnak Deang or Red House, a splendid wooden structure dating from the reign of Rama I but not originally part of the Palace of the Front.

National Museum

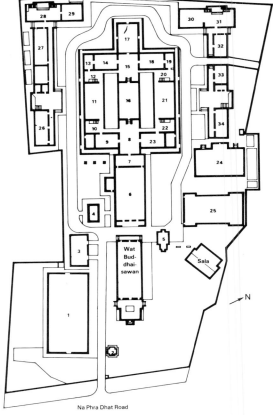

1. Prehistoric findings
2. King Rama VI room
3. The 'Red Palace' room
4. King Rama IV room
5. The Crown Prince room
6. Throne Hall exhibition
7. Gold of Ayutthaya
8. Royal Elephant Regalia
9. Theatrical costumes
10. Royal gifts hall
11. Ceramics, mother of pearl
12. Models
13. Stamps, coins and medals
14. Royal Barges
15. Weapons
16. Royal seals and insignia
17. Wood carvings
18. Boat models
19. Boats and fishing
20. Curiosities
21. Costumes, religious objects
22. Royal fans
23. Musical instruments
24. Old photographs
25. Royal carriages

New South Wing: Lower Level
26. Buddhism in Asia
27. Art of Lopburi
28. Sculpture of Hindu Gods
29. Art of Lopburi

New South Wing: Upper Level
26. Art of Dvaravati period
27. Art of Dvaravati period
28. Javanese sculpture
29. Art of Srivijaya period

New North Wing-Lower Level
30. Coins
31. Buddha Images
32. Textiles
33. Small objets d'art
34. Art of Bangkok period

New North Wing-Upper Level
30. Art of Chiang Saen period
31. Art of Sukhothai period
32. Art of Sukhothai period
33. Art of Ayutthaya period
34. Art of Ayutthaya period

The elaborate doors of Wat Rajabophit represent the religious devotion of their craftsmen, the art performed for religious merit rather than material gain.

Jim Thompson's House (Open Monday to Friday 9 a.m. to 4 p.m. Admission 50 Baht) Located at the end of Soi Kasemsan 2 across from the National Stadium on Rama I Road is the traditional Thai house reconstructed by Mr. Jim Thompson. This remarkable American settled in Bangkok after World War II and went into business to revitalise the local silk industry. In this he was eminently successful and Jim Thompson silk is still one of Bangkok's top buys at the shop he opened at No. 9 Surawong·Road. Thompson achieved legendary status when he disappeared without a trace while on holiday in Malaysia in 1967 - one of the East's greatest modern mysteries.

Besides his interest in silk, Thompson was a great lover of Thai art and antiquities. His house, which is now a museum, is a brilliant example of traditional domestic architecture and was reconstructed by him from six old houses to form an appropriate setting for his beautiful collection of antiques. The house, with its typical *klong*-side location, is an attraction in its own right, while the collection of stone and bronze sculpture, porcelain, woodcarving and paintings is priceless.

Suan Pakkard Palace (Open daily except Sunday 9 a.m. to 4 p.m. Admission 50 Baht) Here, on Sri Ayutthaya Road, is a superb collection of traditional Thai houses set amid extensive landscaped gardens. Belonging to a leading patron of the arts, the attractions include fine old-style architecture, a rare lacquer pavilion (a masterpiece of decorative art), an excellent collection of bronze and stone art works, ceramics and furniture.

Hilton International Hotel on Wireless Road, has perhaps the best landscaped tropical gardens in Bangkok, with a large variety of flowering shrubs and trees. In one corner is the curious shrine dedicated to the female spirit of Chao Mae Tuptim. Considerably pre-dating the hotel, it is, like the Erawan Shrine, popularly believed to be a source of divine assistance. Its peculiarity is that offerings of thanks traditionally take the form of phallic symbols, hundreds of which in all sizes surround the shrine.

Kamthieng House (Open Tuesday-Saturday 9 a.m. to 12 noon and 1 p.m. to 5 p.m. Admission 25 Baht) Located in the compound of the Siam Society (a royal-sponsored association for the promotion of Thai studies) on Soi Asoke (Soi 21), Sukhumvit Road, this old house is a fine example of traditional Northern architecture. It was formerly the home of a prominent family in Chiang Mai until it was donated to the Society. After being dismantled and brought down from the North, it was reconstructed on the present site. Inside is a collection of ethnological artifacts relating to the people and culture of northern Thailand.

Markets

Besides Bangrak and Thieves markets there are a number of old-style retail outlets scattered around the city:

Weekend Market Chatuchak Park, off Phaholyothin Road, near the Northern Bus Terminal. (Open Saturday and Sunday) This is Bangkok's most glorious all-purpose market comprising a staggering array of open-air stalls spread out over an area of roughly 35 acres. The spectrum of merchandise goes from fruit, vegetables and household goods through fabrics, new and secondhand clothing, shoes, toys and tape cassettes to handicrafts, antiques, potted plants, pets of various species and army surplus goods.

Pratunam Market, which spans both sides of Ratchaprarop Road by its intersection with Petchaburi Road, is a market maze specializing in fresh produce, clothing, fabrics and haberdashery.

Tewes Market at the river end of Krung Kasem Road near the National Library, is the best place for flowers and potted plants.

Pak Klong Market at the foot of Memorial Bridge on the Bangkok side, is the city's answer to London's Covent Garden, being the wholesale centre for fruit, vegetables and cut flowers. A lively, colourful place presenting an excellent opportunity for seeing the rich variety of Thailand's fresh produce.

Sanam Luang Bookstalls on the corner of Rajadamnoen Avenue facing Sanam Luang, is the traditional spot for students to pick up secondhand textbooks. Also has a large selection of foreign language paperbacks and magazines.

Thonburi Temples

Wat Arun is the most famous monument on the Thonburi side of the Chao Phraya River, but the following temples are also worth visiting for both their intrinsic interest and their locations close to the riverside.

Wat Kalayanimit near the mouth of Klong Bangkok Yai is easily reached by the cross-river ferry from the Tha Rachini landing stage next to Pak Long Market. This temple, built in the reign of Rama III, is distinguished by its main *viharn* of unusually tall proportions, an architectural feature dictated by the huge statue of the Buddha inside. Wat Kalayanimit is also fascinating for its compound and monks' quarters which, in their riverine setting, give one a sense of how old Bangkok must have looked.

Wat Prayoon a little way downstream from Wat Kalayanimit, beyond Santa Cruz Church, is an attractive temple which is most noted for the small artificial hill to the right of the entrance. It is a charming spot dotted with *chedis* and frangipani trees and surrounded by a pond full of turtles. It was created, so the story goes, after King Rama III noticed one night how the melted wax from his candle formed a curiously shaped mount. He remarked on this to a courtier who later had the hill constructed after the wax model.

Wat Suwannaram and Wat Dusitaram located further upstream near the junction with Klong Bangkok Noi, both have foundations dating from the Ayutthaya period but were reconstructed by King Rama I. The former is an especially good example of the architectural style that bridges the Ayutthaya and Rattanakosin (Bangkok) eras. More striking, however, are the interiors which are decorated with late 18th and early 19th century mural paintings of exceptional quality.

Royal Barges Nearby on Klong Bangkok Noi is the shed housing a collection of highly ornate state barges, including that of the king, formerly used on state ceremonial occasions but today rarely seen. Open daily 8:30 a.m. to 4:30 p.m. Admission 10 Baht.

Waterways and Floating Markets

Most of the *klongs* (canals) on the Bangkok side of the river have been filled in to make way for roads, but in Thonburi many of the old waterways are still in use, and a tour by boat gives a good feel for typical Thai riverine life. The simplest way to cruise along the back canals is to hire your own longtail boat (*hang yao*) from one of the landing stages on the Bangkok side. (Oriental Pier, next to the Oriental Hotel is popular for this, though prices are likely to be higher; try instead the Tha Rachini landing stage near Memorial Bridge. Bargaining is the rule and a reasonable rate for a longtail boat is 150-300 Baht per hour. One boat can comfortably take 6-8 people.)

For longer river trips, the *Oriental Queen*, operated by the Oriental Hotel, runs daily cruises upriver to Ayutthaya and an evening dinner cruise every Wednesday. Tours on this luxury air-conditioned river cruiser can be booked through leading tour agents or at the Oriental.

Alternatively, full-day excursions by public boat to the **Stork Sanctuary** (nesting season is October to April) at Wat Pailom in Pathum Thani, or to Wat Pailongwua in Suphanburi (noted for the weird statuary in its 'Buddhist Park') are operated on Sundays and public holidays, departing between 7 and 8 a.m. from Tha Tien and Tha Maharaj landing stages. Fares are inexpensive. For further details call Chao Phraya Express Boat Co Ltd, tel. 411-0418, or Sukserm Express Boat Service, tel. 211-2296.

Floating Markets The Floating Market (commerce carried out from small sampans) in Thonburi has been over-exposed to tourism and has suffered accordingly. Much more authentic and bigger is the Floating Market at Damnoen Saduak, west of Bangkok. Regular tours are operated daily by leading travel agents. Needs to be visited in the early morning.

Astrologers near Lumpini Park

A monk collecting alms on a canal in Thonburi

The spire of Wat Arun along the Chao Phraya River

Around Bangkok

Rich though Bangkok is in things to do and see, the visitor should allow some time, even on a short stay, to see a little of what lies beyond the capital. The following places can all be covered comfortably on day excursions from Bangkok, either by public transport or, in most cases by organized tours operated daily by leading travel agents (usually bookable through hotel travel counters). These easily accessible attractions range from the ancient capital of Ayutthaya to scenic countryside and glimpses of traditional Thai culture.

North

Ayutthaya

The Thai capital from 1350 to 1767, Ayutthaya is the most important historical site within easy striking distance of Bangkok. Situated on the Chao Phraya river, 85 km. (53 miles) from Bangkok, it can be reached by bus, train or, most luxuriously, by the air-conditioned river cruise *Oriental Queen* which departs daily at 8 a.m. from the Oriental Hotel (the full day tour is one way by boat and one way by tour bus).

Although sacked, looted and razed by Burmese invaders in the 18th century, the surviving ruins of Ayutthaya (the major monuments have been restored as far as possible) stand as testament to the former glory of what was once the most magnificent city in the Orient. In its 17th century heyday it was rich, powerful and proud, a cosmopolitan metropolis where representatives of the major European powers sought to curry favour and seek trade concessions from a court of immense regal splendour.

Ayutthaya is an island city on the Chao Phraya river at its junction with the Pak Sak and Lopburi tributaries, linked by a canal to bring the water all around. The riverine setting survives to this day and an initial exploration around the perimeter waterways of the city can be made by hiring a boat from the landing stage near Chandra Kasem Palace in the northeast corner of town.

Sights

The ruins are scattered around the modern town, a busy little place, though it manages not to obtrude any distractions from the remains of its more illustrious forerunner. Nevertheless it requires a little imagination to picture the original scope and splendour of the former capital. Bear in mind that it was once surrounded by a 12-km. enclosing wall and boasted three major palace complexes and some 400 temples. There were separate quarters, or trading factories, supporting sizeable

communities of foreign residents, both Occidental and Oriental.
Ayutthaya was not only the physical power centre of the nation, it
symbolized the whole concept of nationhood and protected the religious
and cultural traditions of the Thai people. During its 417-year history it
was the capital for 33 kings of five dynasties.

The most important monuments to be seen are:

Wat Phra Sri Sanphet This was the royal temple and originally
stood within the compound of the king's palace. (The latter, comprising
seven buildings, was destroyed by the Burmese and only scattered
foundations remain to give an inkling of its original extent.) Wat Phra Sri
Sanphet, built in 1448 and renovated at least twice, formerly housed a 16
m. Buddha image covered in gold leaf which gave the temple its name.
The statue was ruined in the Burmese attack and today the temple is
distinguished by its row of three *chedis* typical of the Ayutthaya style.

Viharn Phra Mongkol Bopit Close to Wat Phra Sri Sanphet, this
modern building dating from the 1950s enshrines the enormous bronze
Buddha statue of Phra Mongkol Bopit, one of the largest in Thailand.

Wat Phra Ram This temple, a little way southeast of Wat Phra Sri
Sanphet, was first constructed in 1369 by King Ramesuan, the second
monarch of Ayutthaya, on the site where the remains of King U-Thong,
his father, were cremated. It was twice later entirely renovated. The ruins
are dominated by a large central *prang*.

Wat Mahathat On the eastern side of the lake opposite Wat Phra
Ram stand the extensive ruins of Wat Mahathat. The buildings date from
the 14th century and have been severely damaged although the *prang*,
now less than half its original height, is still impressive.

Wat Rachaburana Situated across the road from Wat Mahathat, this
was similarly a large temple complex and is in a better state of
preservation with a particularly fine *prang*. It was built in 1424 by King
Borommaracha II to commemorate his two elder brothers whose ashes
are housed in twin *chedi* still to be seen.

Wat Yanasen & Wat Thammikarat The ruins of these two
temples lie west of Wat Rachaburana. The former is noted for its *chedi*
which, not having suffered from unsatisfactory restoration, is an
especially good example of Ayutthaya workmanship. The ruins of Wat
Thammikarat are also interesting and have an added attraction in their
air of romantic charm.

Wat Na Phra Meru (Phra Mane) Located across the river north of
the site of the Royal Palace, this temple suffered little in the destruction
of 1767 and although restored, its *bot* and *viharn* are attractive buildings.
Of note in the latter structure is a Dvaravati stone Buddha image seated
European fashion with hands on knees, while the *bot* enshrines a good
Ayutthaya style bronze seated Buddha.

Wat Suwan Dhararam Located in the southeast corner of
Ayutthaya, this temple was built by the father of King Rama I shortly

before the fall of the city. Renovated twice (by Rama I and Rama III), it is in excellent condition and is still used. The *bot* has the typical Ayutthaya architectural feature of concave foundations so that the side walls dip in the middle and the interior walls are decorated with mural paintings.

Wat Yai Chai Mongkol & Wat Phanan Choeng These two monuments lie to the southeast but on the opposite side of the river. The former is distinguished by a high *chedi* constructed to commemorate King Naresuan's victory in single-handed, elephant-back combat over the crown prince of Burma in 1592. Wat Phanan Choeng, close to the river banks, is notable in that it is believed to pre-date the founding of Ayutthaya as the capital by 26 years. It enshrines a massive image of the seated Buddha.

Phu Khao Thong (Golden Mount Chedi) This monument lies 2 km. (1.25 miles) outside the city to the northwest and rises imposingly to dominate the surrounding flat countryside. The soaring *chedi* raised on terraces was originally built in Mon style by the Burmese after their first conquest of Ayutthaya in 1569, but the present structure was rebuilt in Thai style by King Borommakot in 1745.

Museums There are two museums in Ayutthaya, the main one being the Chao Sam Phraya Museum in the centre of town on Rojana Road (open Wednesday to Sunday 9 a.m. to noon and 1 p.m. to 4 p.m. Admission 5 Baht). It houses a fine collection of bronze, stone and terracotta statues, mostly from the Ayutthaya period but with some representatives of the Lopburi and U-thong styles, and affords a good introduction to the art of Ayutthaya.

The other, smaller museum is at Chan Kasem Palace in the northeast corner of the city (opening times as above). The building, a museum piece in its own right, stands on the site of the palace where King Naresuan lived before he was crowned, and was reconstructed in the 19th century by King Mongkut. It occupies a pleasant compound with gardens, a tranquil oasis compared to the busy street outside.

Bang Pa-In

On the Chao Phraya River a few kilometres downstream from Ayutthaya is the former royal summer retreat of Bang Pa-In (open daily except Monday, 8:30 a.m. to noon and 1 p.m. to 4 p.m. Admission 10 Baht). The palace comprises a collection of buildings in a surprising variety of architectural styles - Thai, Chinese, Italian, Victorian - which, enhanced by the grounds and ornamental ponds, possess a certain picture-postcard charm.

Bang Pa-In was first used by the kings of Ayutthaya in the 17th century, although it fell into disuse after the Burmese invasion of 1767 and the buildings seen today date from the late 19th and early 20th centuries.

The palace no longer serves as a royal retreat during the hot season and is rarely used. Nevertheless, the only building open to the public is the ornate Chinese-style Vehat Chamroon Palace. This and the Thai-style Aisawan Tippaya Asna pavilion, enchantingly raised over a pond, are the two most striking buildings in the complex.

Bang Pa-In can be reached by bus, car or, most pleasantly, by boat from Ayutthaya. It is also included in the *Oriental Queen's* Ayutthaya cruise.

Lopburi

This historically important town north of Ayutthaya on the Lopburi River 153 km. (95 miles) from Bangkok is not yet well-established on the tourist itinerary but is very much worth visiting and a must for anyone interested in 17th century Thai history.

Originally called Louvo, it was already an important town during the Dvaravati and Khmer periods. It reached its zenith during the reign of King Narai (1656-1688) who made it the 'second city' of Ayutthaya and used it for all intents and purposes as the kingdom's capital.

It was here that the major events of the most exciting episodes of Narai's reign were played out. The king's chief minister, the remarkable Greek, Constance Phaulkon, built his residence at Lopburi, close to Narai's palace where the French embassy headed by Chevalier de Chaumont was received in 1685.

The height of intrigue and the last moments of Lopburi's glory came in 1688 when Phra Petracha led a palace revolution and violently established a new ruling dynasty. King Narai was, fortunately for him, dying of natural causes, but his heirs were murdered and Phaulkon, holding the greatest power any foreigner has ever achieved in Thailand, was executed on charges (arguably trumped up) of treason. After taking the throne Petracha reestablished royal residence at Ayutthaya and Lopburi fell into decline.

Sights

Today the town is the provincial capital and a sizeable army base; its modern appearance is not inspiring. Nevertheless, scattered among the latter-day development (and well worth exploring) are some excellent ruins attesting to the rich and eventful past.

The major sights, taken in historical order, are:

Phra Prang Sam Yot Located in the centre of the old town on a grassy mound next to the railway crossing is the classic monument to Lopburi's Khmer heritage. Built in the 13th century it comprises three *prangs* linked by a central corridor and is a good and well preserved example of Khmer architecture indicative of the Bayon style. The huge laterite blocks were once covered with stucco and a few traces of this decoration can still be seen. Originally constructed as a Hindu shrine, Phra Prang Sam Yot was later used as a Buddhist temple and two of the towers contain partially ruined Buddha statues in the Lopburi style. In front to the east is a brick *viharn* probably built in the reign of King Narai.

San Phra Khan Across the railway tracks from Phra Prang Sam Yot and enclosed as the centre of a traffic circle is another monument of the Khmer period. To be seen is the laterite base of what originally must have been a massive *prang,* but this no longer exists and the distinguishing feature of the site is an unimpressive shrine housing an image of the Hindu god Kala. The area is overrun by a troop of monkeys seemingly possessed of all the bad and none of the good traits of their kind.

Prang Khaek Situated in a square in the middle of town this is another Khmer relic, a Hindu sanctuary comprising the fairly well preserved ruins of a central tallish tower and two smaller flanking *prangs*. Made of brick, it has been restored although stylistic influence suggesting the Angkor period indicate it could have been first constructed in the 10th century.

Wat Phra Si Ratana Mahathat (Open daily 8:30 a.m. to 4 a.m. Admission 20 Baht) This is Lopburi's single most impressive and important religious ruin, located in the southern part of town opposite the railway station.

The origins of the temple complex, which covers an area of 3 hectares, are unknown although it is certain that it spans the Khmer period and Narai's reign. The ruins are dominated by a large laterite Khmer *prang* which was probably originally constructed in the 12th century and remodelled in the 14th. The superb structure shows Bayon influences in the surviving traces of stucco decoration, but its design is untypical and so it is thought the building seen today dates from the time when the Thais were beginning to overshadow the Khmer in the region.

The other principal feature, the large brick *viharn*, was clearly built in the reign of King Narai and displays Western and Persian styles in its pointed arch windows.

Surrounding are indications of cloisters and the remains of enclosing walls, while dotting the entire site are a number of *chedis* and *prangs*, some of which have been well restored and are of considerable stylistic interest.

Taken in their entirety the ruins of Wat Phra Si Ratana Mahathat possess both historical value and a mantle of charm and elegance. The trip to Lopburi is rewarding for this monument alone.

Phra Narai Rajanivet (The Palace of King Narai) (Open Wednesday to Sunday 9 a.m. to noon and 1 p.m. to 4 p.m. Admission 20 Baht) The huge battlements of the palace built by King Narai between 1665 and 1677 dominate the western side of town close to the banks of the Lopburi River. The main approach was once by water but now a row of buildings impede direct access to the river. A number of gateways, topped by unusual pointed arches, pierce the walls at intervals and the main entrance is via the Pratu (gate) Phayakkha on Sorasak Road. The latter is presumably named after Luang Sorasak, son of Phra Petracha, who hated Phaulkon and, when Narai was dying, set a trap and captured the Greek as he was entering the palace via this gate. Phaulkon was then imprisoned and tortured for a few days until one night he was led out of the palace on elephant back and taken to his place of execution.

Partially designed by French architects, the palace buildings have an originality of style and were laid out in three compounds, formerly separated by inner walls. The first area was devoted to government buildings, the second to ceremonial buildings and the inner compound to Narai's private residence. An interesting feature on the inside of some of the walls are the rows of niches that would have contained oil lamps on ceremonial occasions, doubtless creating an impressive sight.

After the death of Narai, Petracha remained in Lopburi only long enough for his coronation and then abandoned the place in favour of Ayutthaya. The palace fell into disrepair and then ruins until the 19th century when King Mongkut restored part of it and added his own pavilion (in a mix of Thai, Chinese and European styles).

Today most of the 17th century buildings are completely ruined, although the palace grounds are well tended and maintained as a kind of public park.

In the first courtyard as you enter there are on the left the remains of storehouses and a reservoir and, at the far end, what survives of the elephant stables. In the adjacent quadrangle to the left are the ruins of the reception hall and the Phra Chao Hao building, which may have once enshrined an important Buddha image.

Further inside, in the northwest quadrangle are traces of the Suttha Sawan Pavilion where Narai died. In the heart of the palace, next to Mongkut's pavilion, is the Chanthara Phisan, constructed by Narai and restored in the 19th century. Behind these two buildings was the closed-in royal harem. Left to Mongkut's pavilion (as you face it) are the ruins of the Dusit Sawan Thanya Maha Prasat, formerly used for receiving foreign ambassadors and where de Chaumont delivered the famous letter from King Louis XIV in 1685 during his audience with Narai. The pavilion built by King Mongkut now serves as a museum and contains a small but stunning collection of Lopburi style sculpture and other artifacts.

Wat Sao Thong Thong Situated directly north of Narai's palace, close to the river, this temple is noted for its *viharn* which was originally a Christian chapel during the Narai period and later converted to Buddhist use. The other old buildings in the compound also date from the Narai period and were once used as residences by the ambassadors from Persia.

Phaulkon's House (Open daily 8:30 a.m. to 4 p.m. Admission 20 Baht) The residence built by Constance Phaulkon, or Chao Phraya Wichayen (the title conferred by King Narai), stands across the street from Wat Sao Thong Thong. Within the walled compound can be seen the fairly substantial ruins of three main buildings: on the west Phaulkon's house itself; in the centre a Catholic church and residence of the Jesuits and, on the east side, the accommodation constructed for members of the 1685 French mission. The brick and cement edifices are a weird blend of architectural styles in which European predominates, but not to the total exclusion of Thai influences.

Wat Tong Pou This 400-year-old temple, located a little way north of San Phra Khan, off the street which cuts through the northeast corner of the old town, is less well known than the other sights of Lopburi and is undeservedly neglected by visitors. To be seen are a venerable *bot*, with a two-tier tiled roof, an equally old *viharn*, a small library and a little bell tower with some stucco decoration. The *bot* and the *viharn* contain a number of Buddha images, most in the Lopburi style, and the compound is dotted with several old small *chedis*.

Northeast

Wang Takrai Park

This is one of Thailand's finest parks and is the perfect destination for a day trip into the countryside. It is best covered by hiring your own car and driver in Bangkok.

Encompassing 80 hectares, Wang Takrai was created in 1955 by the late Prince Chumbot of Nagara Svarga and subsequently opened to the public by his widow who has continued to develop the landscaped gardens. Situated in a picturesque valley 106 km. (66 miles) from Bangkok, the park is traversed by a stream and is planted with a large variety of trees, shrubs and flowers.

Additional attractions nearby include the sanctuary of Chao Po Khun Dan which commemorates an officer of that name who served under King Naresuan (reigned 1590-1605) and whose spirit is believed to guard the surrounding mountains; and two waterfalls, Nam Rong and Salika (best seen at the end of the rainy season).

The closest main town of Wang Takrai is Nakhon Nayok on highway 305. At the town you take highway 33 until its intersection with highway 3049. Here you turn left and after 11 km. you reach a fork in the road; right leads to Wang Takrai (2 km.) and Nam Rong waterfall (7 km.) while straight on takes you to Salika waterfall.

Khao Yai National Park

Khao Yai, 205 km. (127 miles) from Bangkok is the closest hill country resort to the capital. It is reached by taking Highway 1 from Bangkok to the outskirts of Saraburi where you turn east on to Highway 2 ("Friendship Highway"). About 58 km. (36 miles) beyond Saraburi, just before the little town of Pak Chong, a signposted turnoff on the right leads just over 20 km. (13 miles) to the park entrance (admission 25 Baht per car).

The 3-4 hour journey is best covered by hiring your own car and driver in Bangkok. Alternatively public buses leave the Northeastern Bus Terminal on Phaholyothin Road every hour for Pak Chong where minibuses ply the last part of the route to the park.

Khao Yai is Thailand's best known wildlife and nature preserve and covers 542,000 acres of protected forest, jungle and grassland spread over rolling hills and mountains (the highest peak, Khao Laem, is

1,328 m. (4,357 ft.) above sea level). It is an area of impressive natural beauty, and the mountain vantage points offer spectacular panoramic views over densely forested valleys and hillsides. Adding to the scenic attractions are a number of waterfalls, one of which, Heo Suwat, tumbles dramatically 15 m. (50 ft.) into a deep, wooded glen.

Protected within the park are bears, tigers, elephants, monkeys, wild hogs, mouse deer, sambar deer, barking deer, porcupines, civets and mongooses, along with various species of birds and butterflies. The later are to be seen in abundance, but you'll need a good deal of luck to catch sight of the rarer animals.

Khao Yai has been wonderfully laid out to afford maximum access and full appreciation of the breathtaking scenery and refreshingly cooler temperatures. A paved road cuts north-south through the park, with branch roads to Heo Suwat waterfall and to near the summit of Khao Kaeo mountain. In addition there is an extensive network of hiking trails (maps provided by the park service) and an 18-hole golf course.

Accommodation is available at the Khao Yai Motor Lodge which offers motel rooms (from 380 Baht) and bungalows (from 600 Baht) plus a camping site and dormitory rooms. The lodge is operated by the Tourism Authority of Thailand with whom reservations should be made in advance in Bangkok (tel. 282-1143-7).

Southeast

Crocodile Farm (Open daily 8 a.m. to 6 p.m. Admission 80 Baht, children half-price) 30 km. (19 miles) from Bangkok. What is claimed as the world's largest crocodile farm - it has some 30,000 reptiles - was established in 1950 with the aim of saving the species from extinction and, at the same time, ensuring a supply of skins for the leather trade. It has subsequently expanded into a very tourist orientated mini-zoo with tigers, deer, monkeys, snakes and elephants. There are also hourly shows of crocodile wrestling (both the crocs and the keeper have been doing it for years and seem a little weary) and elephant shows. Feeding time is between 5 and 6 p.m.

Ancient City (Open daily 8:30 a.m. to 6 p.m. Admission 50 Baht, children half-price) This open-air museum located 3 km. (2 miles) from the Crocodile Farm occupies a 200-acre site shaped to the outline of Thailand and comprises an excellent collection of full and smaller-scale replicas of the country's major monuments and temples. Each building is situated according to its actual geographic location to give an idea of regional variations in architectural style. A few structures are original and have been relocated for preservation at the Ancient City; some others are reproductions of buildings which no longer exist, such as the Grand Palace of Ayutthaya. There is also a model Thai village.

The Ancient City may sound like a typical tourist trap but, in fact, the monuments have been faithfully reproduced in full detail and do give a genuine insight into the nation's architectural heritage.

Pattaya

Pattaya, located 145 km. (95 miles) southwest of Bangkok, is oft dubbed "Queen of Asia's Resorts"; in fact it is in a class of its own, almost defying succinct description. Let it be said straight away, it is not to everyone's liking. It is like nowhere else: brash, bawdy, colourful and alive with activity. It is arrogant and self-assured in its kaleidoscope of watersports and shore-based entertainment that almost make the beach superfluous and ensure there is never a dull moment - day or night.

In little more than two decades what was once an untouched, gently curving bay bordered by an unpaved road with a tiny fishing village at one end has grown up into Thailand's premier beach resort and an international playground. First, a string of deluxe hotels sprang up along the shore line. Then followed a largely unorganized building boom with more hotels, bars, restaurants and shops spreading back well inland from the beach. At the same time sporting and recreational facilities - orthodox and unorthodox - appeared in a star-burst of activity designed to get the visitor on, above and below the water and keep him (much is male orientated) fully occupied on land.

Today, construction extends in all possible directions and the beach is scarcely any longer the focal point. For the simple pleasures of sun, sea and sand, people really need to venture a short distance south to Jomtien Beach, just around the headland and virtually an annex of Pattaya.

This irrepressible resort can be whatever you want to make of it. Its frenetic development has been characterized by an all-out attempt to offer the best of everything in an unparalleled mix of facilities. Nowhere else has to the same degree such a full spectrum of sporting activities, nightlife attractions, shopping amenities and a complete range of hotels and restaurants to suit all tastes and all pockets.

Although Pattaya is pretty much of a muchness, there is some variation. At the north end of the resort there are some comparatively quiet beaches and coves, such as Moonlight Beach, where one can rent bungalows and enjoy a fairly tranquil time. Stretching south is the long bay with the main beach and a parallel road fronted by mostly deluxe hotels. Behind the main coast road is Pattaya 2nd Road (the back road), the two being connected by numerous sois (lanes) and the whole area being considerably built-up. At the southern end of the bay is what used to be the fishing village and is now popularly referred to as "The Strip". Crammed into a small space are a jumble of open-air bars, go-go bars, discos, restaurants and shops. This is the nighttime (and much of the daytime) entertainment centre, largely geared to the desires of the single male. Even if this bawdy scene is not to one's liking, "The Strip" is worth visiting just to see it as a phenomenon and indulge in the pleasant pastime of people-watching.

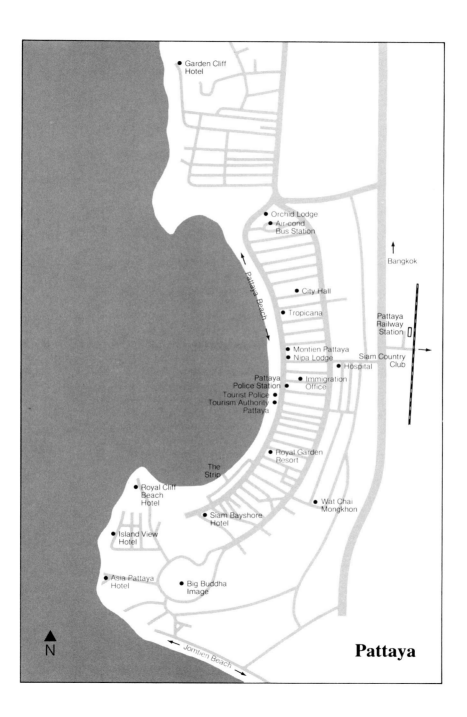

Garden Cliff
Hotel

Orchid Lodge
Air-cond
Bus Station

Bangkok

City Hall

Tropicana

Pattaya
Railway
Station

Montien Pattaya
Nipa Lodge
Hospital

Siam Country
Club

Pattaya
Police Station
Tourist Police
Tourism Authority
Pattaya

Immigration
Office

Royal Garden
Resort

The
Strip

Royal Cliff
Beach
Hotel

Wat Chai
Mongkhon

Siam Bayshore
Hotel

Island View
Hotel

Asia Pattaya
Hotel

Big Buddha
Image

Pattaya Beach

N

Jomtien Beach

Pattaya

Up on the southern headland are two or three more deluxe hotels. The best is the Royal Cliff which has its own beach and watersports facilities. This could be described as the more select area of Pattaya.

While the visitor can simply laze by his hotel pool and sip on a long cool drink, there is nevertheless an irresistible pull towards a staggering range of sporting options:

Parasailing offers thrills and great views as you dangle from a parachute towed along by a speed boat. Individual operators are found on Pattaya and Jomtien beaches and charge 200-250 Baht for a flight over the bay lasting 2-3 minutes.

Windsurfing is very popular at all beaches, though best at Jomtien. Hire of board and sail costs around 100 Baht per hour, or 300 Baht per day. Lessons may also be taken at one of several windsurfing schools.

Scuba Diving is good in the comparatively clear water and with a fair amount of coral and tropical fish to be seen. A number of dive shops in Pattaya offer tuition ranging from one-day courses to a full certificate course. These shops also rent scuba equipment.

Sailing is best at Jomtien Beach where Hobiecats and Prindles can be hired for 300-400 Baht per hour.

Deep-Sea Fishing The main centre for game fishing expeditions is Bang Saray, 18 km. (11 miles) south of Pattaya, where Fisherman's Inn and Fisherman's Lodge organize trips and provide the gear for going after shark, barracuda and marlin.

Waterskiing Speedboats can be hired at various beach locations for upwards of 700 Baht per hour.

Waterscooters These machines are a pest and dangerous. Their use is officially limited to certain points of Pattaya and Jomtien beaches. Can be a rip-off as some scooters are clapped out and malfunctions may be charged to the hirer.

Tennis Many leading hotels have their own tennis courts.

Golf There is a good 18-hole, 72 par course at the Siam Country Club (facilities also at Bang Phra and the Royal Thai Navy course). All three links are about a half-hour drive from Pattaya. Check with your hotel reception or tour counter for details of fees, transport, etc.

Shooting & Archery are available at Pattaya Sport Bazaar Bldg, 2nd Pattaya Road. Tel: 419642, 421700-3. Pistols (.22, .38 and 9mm) and .22 rifles can be hired and range fee is 120 Baht per person with bullets costing 39 Baht depending on calibre. There is also an outdoor archery range where a bow and 30 arrows cost 100 Baht. Open 11 a.m. to 10 p.m.

Bowling & Snooker Pattaya Bowl, 2nd Pattaya Road. Tel: 419466. Also at Simon Bowl, 2nd Pattaya Road.

Horseback Riding at Reo Park Range on Siam Country Club Road, 5km. (3 miles) from the Sukhumvit Highway. For beginners and experienced riders. Rates from 350 Baht per hour.

After sundown there is no discernable change of pace and the choice of evening activities almost rivals that of the day - restaurants serving fresh seafood and a host of national cuisines; bars with or without go-go dancers; massage parlours, discos and, in the major hotels, rather more sedate nightclubs with live music.

A particular speciality of Pattaya's entertainment scene are transvestite shows with men impersonating famous female singers and performing song and dance routines in cabaret spectacles. The two top spots are Tiffany's on Pattaya 2nd Road and Alcazar Cabaret, which is nearby.

There is just one thing Pattaya makes no claim to offer - peace and quiet. There is no attempt to provide an escape from the bustle of modern living, and instead the resort thrives on a carnival atmosphere. Nevertheless Pattaya is not all a brash bachelor's paradise, and there are a number of nearby attractions that offer alternatives to the usual resort fare, especially for family groups.

Around Pattaya

Islands One of the easiest alternatives to the frenetic activity of Pattaya is to make a trip out to one of the offshore islands. Most popular, and now well developed, is Koh Larn, 10 km. (6 miles) from Pattaya, to which day tours are organized at 250 Baht per head. Further off and less built up is Koh Phai to which the return boat fare is about 400 Baht.

Nong Nooch Village (Open daily. Cultural show 3-4:30 p.m.) Located 15 minutes drive from Pattaya at km 165 Sukhumvit Highway, this is a country resort comprising a collection of traditional Thai-style cottages set amid rolling hills and extensive landscaped gardens. Attractions include a cultural show, elephant show, mini zoo, boating on the lake, orchid nurseries and cactus garden.

Elephant Kraal (Open daily. Show 3-5 p.m. Admission 160 Baht) The place to see how elephants are captured and trained for work in the teak forests of the North, plus demonstrations of pachyderm skills and elephant rides. Popular with children. The Elephant Kraal is a short distance inland from the resort, just off the Sukhumvit Highway.

Khao Khieo Open Zoo (Open daily 7 a.m. to 6 p.m. Admission adults 20 Baht, children 10 Baht.) Situated about 24 km. (15 miles) off the main highway from the turn off to Bang Phra Golf Course near Bang Saen, this open zoo (actually the animals are fenced in but have far more space to move around than usual) has elephants, bears, zebras, deer of various species, monkeys, wild boars and more, plus numerous kinds of birds housed in an enormous aviary. The hilly setting and woodland scenery are extremely attractive and add to the pleasure of this interesting attraction.

Bang Saen Aquarium (Open daily 9 a.m. to 5 p.m. Admission 10 Baht, children half price) The coastal town of Bang Saen, just off the main highway about 45 km. (30 miles) north of Pattaya, is an older beach resort and still popular with Thais for day and weekend excursions. Its main point of interest for the international visitor, however, is the Aquarium and Natural History Museum at Srinakharinwirot University, on the left on the way into town.

Chanthaburi Gem Mines Day excursions can be made to the gem mining area around the town of Chanthaburi, 185 km. (115 miles) southeast of Pattaya. Fine quality sapphires in particular are found here and the open pit mines can be visited as can the gem cutting factories in town. The region is also known for its picturesque scenery and fruit cultivation.

Organized tours are operated to several of the above places. Check with your hotel tour counter for full details.

Getting to Pattaya

Several private bus companies operate regular daily services between Bangkok and Pattaya, the best known being Diamond Coach at 1494 New Petchburi Road, tel. 252-4248-51, which has three departures in each direction a day at 8:30 a.m., 12:30 p.m. and 5 p.m. One way fare is 120 Baht. Bookings can be made at the tour counters of leading hotels from which pick-up services are offered. Alternatively the government owned Bor Kor Sor bus company has departures every 30 minutes between 6:30 a.m. and 8:30 p.m. from the Ekamai Bus Terminal on Sukhumvit Road near Soi 42. One-way fare is 50 Baht.

In Pattaya the easiest way to get around is by *song taew*, minibus pick-up trucks which ply the main roads and stop on request. Fares within the beach area should be around 5 Baht and between 20-30 Baht for longer journeys.

Southwest

Samut Sakhon

Also known as Mahachai, Samut Sakhon is a typical picturesque fishing port located 28 km. (17 miles) from Bangkok at the junction of the Tachin River and the Mahachai Canal by the Gulf of Thailand. It is interesting for its busy scene, its fish market and, by the main landing stage, a restaurant serving excellent seafood. A boat may also be hired from the fish market pier for a trip to the port's principal temple, Wat Chom Long, at the mouth of the Tachin River.

In addition to its intrinsic charm, Samut Sakhon is the destination of an unusual excursion. A narrow-gauge railway runs from Wong Wian Yai station in Thonburi (near the Taksin Monument) to the port, and the delightful hour-long journey passes through some very pleasant wetland scenery. Departures are approximately every hour.

Hua Hin

Located 188 km. (117 miles) south of Bangkok on the western coast of the Gulf of Thailand, more or less opposite Pattaya, is Hua Hin, Thailand's oldest beach resort, which offers a quieter alternative to its younger and more brash counterpart across the Gulf.

Long known as a busy fishing port, Hua Hin first came to prominence as a resort in the 1920s when Rama VII established a Royal Summer Palace there (it is still used by the present King.) A vogue was thus established and the then first class Railway Hotel, built in charming colonial style, was opened to cater to a burgeoning vacation traffic.

Some time after World War II Hua Hin went into decline as a resort - the Railway Hotel languishing along with it - and it was not until the mid 1980s, when the deluxe Royal Garden Resort Hotel was built, that the beach town once again came into fashion.

The old Railway Hotel, now known as the Hotel Sofitel, is located only a short distance away from its modern rival. It maintains its 1920s charm while providing up-to-date facilities.

While these two properties provide international standard accommodation and Hua Hin is now back on the tourist map, the resort as yet shows no signs of going the same way as Pattaya: it is still a place mainly for quiet family vacations.

The main attraction is the beach, mostly undeveloped except for some ponies to ride and some watersports facilities offered by the Royal Garden Resort. Otherwise Hua Hin's sporting attraction is golf, on a good 18 hole course.

The town goes about its business with scarcely a regard for the tourist. It is interesting for its fishing port, its bustling night bazaar and a handful of simple restaurants serving the local seafood. The place is small enough to walk around although trishaws are a plentiful and inexpensive means of transport. Most tourist activity is concentrated around the two main hotels, just south of the town centre, but there are no sights as such, except for the quaint railway station with its royal waiting room which must be one of the most attractive little stations anywhere.

Sights

Should the visitor not be content with lazing on the beach, enjoying a few rounds of golf or strolling around town, the surrounding district does have touring possibilities. The hinterland is one of picturesque hills, jungle, lakes, sugar cane and pineapple plantations, while the continuing coastline is most attractive.

For the culturally oriented, the historic town of **Phetburi**, 65 km. (40 miles) north, is worth a few hours. A centre of artistic output during the Ayutthaya period, it boasts a handful of beautiful old temples (note the superb mural paintings in Wat Yai Suwannaram and Wat Ko Keo Suttharam) a hilltop palace built by King Mongkut, and Khao Luang Cave, which enshrines a number of Buddha images.

South of Hua Hin 23 km. (14 miles) away, is the port of Pran Buri and close by the national park of **Khao Sam Roi Yot** ("Mountain of 300 Peaks"). The latter is a magnificent place, comprising forested hills, waterfalls, caves, beaches and coves, and a profusion of flora and fauna. Of particular note among the caves is Phraya Nakhon where a shrine has been erected to commemorate a visit by King Rama V.

Getting to Hua Hin

Diamond Coach Service (Bangkok tel. 252-4248/51) operates a daily airconditioned bus service, departing Bangkok at 9 a.m. and taking about 3.5 hours. (The same bus stops at Cha-Am.) In the opposite direction, the bus leaves Hua Hin at 2:30 p.m. Round-trip fare is 350 Baht. Alternatively, government run buses leave the Southern Bus Terminal in Thonburi every hour. There are also daily trains from Bangkok Railway Station.

West

Rose Garden (Open daily 8 a.m. to 6 p.m. Admission to gardens 10 Baht; to Cultural Show 140 Baht) Located on the banks of the Tachin River 32km. (20 miles) from Bangkok and set amid lovely landscaped gardens, this is both a country resort (with a good standard of accommodation) and day attraction in its model Thai village and cultural show. The latter, every afternoon at 3, has displays of folk dances, sword fighting, traditional ceremonies and similar examples of old-style Thai culture. In the village are work elephants and workshops for various local handicrafts. It is all a little 'instant Thailand' in character, but it is well done and good for visitors with only a short time to spend in the country.

As a country resort, the Rose Garden has tennis courts, a swimming pool, an artificial lake with paddle boats and an 18-hole golf course.

Daily organized tours from Bangkok include the Rose Garden, along with Damnoen Saduak Floating Market and Nakhon Pathom (see below).

Nakhon Pathom

This town, 56 km. (35 miles) from Bangkok, stands on the site of one of the oldest settlements in what is now Thailand and is widely believed to have been the earliest centre of Buddhist learning in the country. Habitation of the area possibly dates back to the 3rd century BC and the city was the capital of a Mon kingdom during the Dvaravati period (6th-11th century).

Sights

Dominating the modern town is the **Phra Pathom Chedi,** the world's tallest Buddhist monument at 127 m. (417 ft.). It marks the location of an ancient *chedi* constructed during the early Dvaravati period and then partially destroyed in 1057 when the city was sacked by King Aniruddha of Pagan.

It was not until the 19th century that King Mongkut re-evaluated the ruins and decided to restore them. However, the original structure, then standing at 40 m. (131 ft.), proved to be beyond repair and Mongkut ordered a new *chedi* to be built over the ruins, the work being completed in the reign of King Chulalongkorn.

Phra Pathom Chedi is distinguished by its ringed cone atop a massive orange glazed tile base in the shape of an inverted bowl. The proportions of the latter are so great as to belie the true height of the structure.

Located in a vast park in the centre of town, this impressive monument stands on a series of terraces and is surrounded by cloisters with chapels at the four cardinal points. There are various other embellishments to the site, including a replica of the original *chedi*, while on the south side is a museum (open Wednesday to Sunday 9 a.m. to noon and 1 to 4 p.m.) which contains some interesting Dvaravati exhibits.

A three-day temple fair is held every November in the grounds of the Phra Pathom Chedi. It is a colourful and lively affair with foodstalls, sideshows and other kinds of traditional entertainment.

The other main attraction in Nakhon Pathom is **Sanam Chand Palace**, on the west side of town. It was built as a summer residence by King Vajiravudh (Rama VI) and presents a most curious mix of English and Thai architectural styles. It is now used as government offices and is not open to the public. However, the gardens, where there is a renovated Thai *sala*, may be visited.

Kanchanaburi

Kanchanaburi, main town of the province of the same name, is best known as the location of the infamous Death Railway and Bridge over the River Kwai constructed by Allied prisoners of the Japanese during World War II. The bridge still exists while other reminders of this grim period of history are to be found in two war cemeteries and a small war museum.

Although most visitors make just a day excursion to see the bridge, Kanchanaburi is not without more pleasurable attractions, and many regard the province as having some of the most beautiful natural scenery to be found in the country.

Kanchanaburi can be reached by bus or train with several daily departures from the Southern Bus Terminal (on Charan Sanitwong Road) and Hualampong Station.

Leading Bangkok travel agents operate one-day excursions from Bangkok which take in the River Kwai Bridge and other sights near town. Longer tours with accommodation at jungle resorts are also offered.

One of the best one-day excursions is the rail trip operated by the State Railways of Thailand on weekends. The special train departs Hualampong at 6:15 a.m. on Saturdays and Sundays and stops at Nakhon Pathom, Kanchanaburi and Nam Tok with ample time for sightseeing at each location.

The town of Kanchanaburi stands 129 km. (80 miles) from Bangkok, at the point where the Kwai Yai and Kwai Noi rivers meet to form the Mae Klong River. Both valleys are extremely picturesque and are dotted with waterfalls and caves. The general landscape is one of lush wooded hills with an impressive backdrop of the rugged, saw-tooth mountains that form the border with Burma. There are a number of popular scenic spots in both valleys and several 'jungle' resort hotels offering good accommodation and opportunities for river trips and jungle treks.

Sights

Kanchanaburi is not an old town - it was built under royal patronage in the reign of King Rama III - but it is a prosperous little place deriving a good income from sugar cane, sapphire mining and the teak trade with Burma. Apart from the bridge and one or two other sights, it offers nothing spectacular although it does have a pleasant, restful atmosphere - an evening stroll along the river front and dinner in one of the little floating Thai restaurants is an enjoyable experience if you are staying overnight.

River Kwai Bridge After the film and the novel, the bridge over the River Kwai can appear less awesome and smaller than expected; it remains nonetheless an important historical monument. Located 5 km. (3 miles) north of the town centre, the bridge is still in use (although the end of the line is only a few kilometres away), by pedestrians as well as by the little train.

During World War II the Japanese aimed to complete a rail link between Burma and Thailand (which they occupied ostensibly with the approval of the Thai government), and the bridge spanning the River

Kwai was a crucial sector. Materials were brought from Java and it is estimated that as many as 216,000 POWs and 49,000 civilian forced labourers died from disease, malnutrition and harsh treatment during the rush to complete the railway.

The bridge was bombed towards the end of the war and only the curved spans seen today are original (the straight ones were later replacements for bomb damage). After hostilities ended the railway was purchased by the Thai government, although by that time the British had begun dismantling the track at the Burmese border and the line now ends at Nam Tok station, about 60 km. (38 miles) from Kanchanaburi.

Kanchanaburi has two cemeteries containing the remains of Allied prisoners of war who perished during the construction of the Death Railway. The **Kanchanaburi War Cemetery** is on Saengchuto Road (Kanchanaburi's main street), opposite and a little way before the railway station. Here there are the graves of 6,982 POWs. The other, **Chungkai War Cemetery**, lies to the south of town on the opposite bank of the Kwai Noi about 3 km. (2 miles) from the ferry landing stage. It stands on the former site of the Chungkai POW Camp and contains the remains of some 1,750 Allied soldiers.

Located in the compound of Wat Chai Chumpol, is the **Jeath War Museum** (Open daily 8:30 a.m. to 4 p.m. Admission 20 Baht). This curious little museum was built to resemble POW camp accommodation. Its exhibits of mostly photographs and paintings by prisoners tell the story of the conditions endured during the construction of the railway.

Wat Tham Mangkhon Thong Best known of Kanchanaburi's cave temples, the "Cave Temple of the Golden Dragon" lies southwest of town on the peninsula between the Kwai Noi and Mae Klong rivers a couple of kilometres from the southern most ferry point.

The main temple buildings are clustered at the foot of a hill situated a few hundred metres off to the left of the road. Next to the *viharn* is a small round pool in which an elderly nun meditates while floating on her back (weekends only, at 10 a.m.).

From the temple compound a steep flight of steps leads up the limestone hill to a cave in front of which sits a Chinese hermit. There are two altars with Buddha images and behind the front one a narrow illuminated tunnel cuts through the mountain to exit a little further up. The passage is low and you have to crawl in places - not for the claustrophobic.

Two other cave temples that can be visited are Wat Tham Khao Laem, a half-mile or so before Wat Tham Mangkhon Thong, and Wat Tham Kao Poon which lies about a ten-minute walk beyond Chungkai War Cemetery.

Bor-Ploy Sapphire Mines Blue sapphires found here are considered to be among the best in the world. Bor-Ploy is about 50 km. (30 miles) north of Kanchanaburi (can be reached by bus or car) and

visitors may view the openpit mine in operation.

Waterfalls and Caves

The valleys of both the Kwai Yai and Kwai Noi are dotted with waterfalls and caves several of which have been groomed as local scenic spots and are popular picnic sites. The waterfalls are more picturesque than spectacular and are best seen at the end of the rainy season.

Erawan Waterfall in a national park is located in the Kwai Yai valley about 70 km. (43.5 miles) from Kanchanaburi. For many Thais it is the most beautiful in the region and has seven levels with pools in between that are ideal for swimming. Note: it can get very crowded with picnickers especially at weekends.

Khao Phang or Sai Yok Noi Waterfall is located about 2 km. (1.5 miles) from Nam Tok railways station in the Kwai Noi valley and can be reached by train from Kanchanaburi.

Kaeng Lawa Cave and Sai Yok Yai Waterfall lie further up the Kwai Noi and can be reached by boat from the Pak Saeng pier near Nam Tok. The trip, which costs 600-800 Baht per boat (carries 10-12 passengers) takes 2.5 hours on the way up and 1.5 hours coming downstream. Kaeng Lawa is the biggest cave in the area, and the journey is well worthwhile for the overall beauty of the scenery.

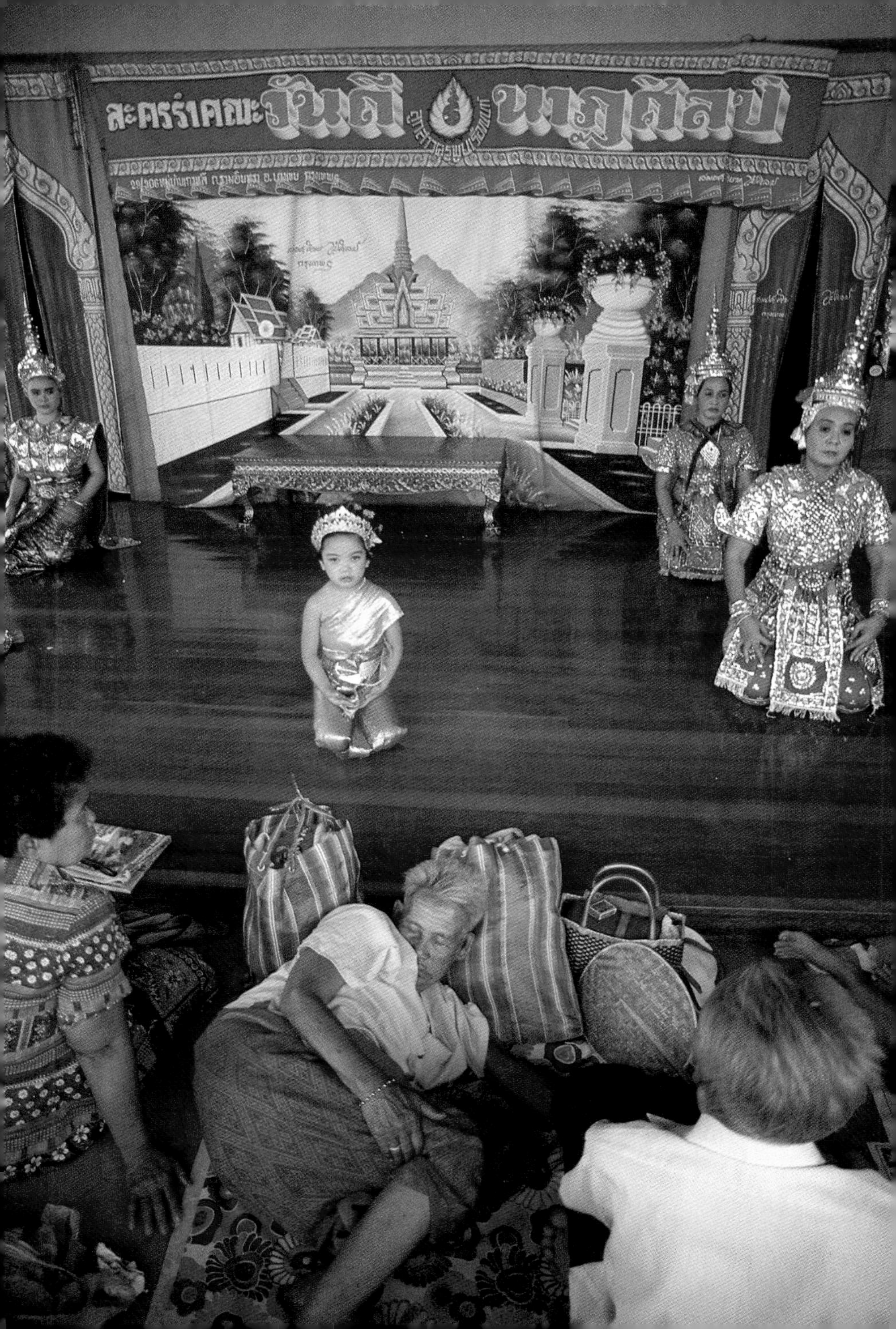
ละครรำคณะ วันดี นาฏศิลป์

Major Thai Festivals and Holidays

Festivals are an essential part of Thai life and the national calendar is dotted with many special events and public holidays. Some are secular, some are Buddhist but most are colourful, joyous affairs, occasions for celebrating and having a good time. Many festivals follow the lunar calendar and thus are "moveable" feasts, while others have set annual dates. The following are the most important yearly celebrations.

January

New Year's Day — January 1 is an official Thai holiday though celebrations are international rather than specifically Thai in flavour.

February

Makha Bucha — Falling on the day of the full moon, this important Buddhist holiday commemorates the occasion when 1,250 disciples gathered spontaneously to hear the Buddha speak. The day of merit-making ends with candlelit processions around temples.

Kite Flying — February is the start of the kite flying season which runs until April.

April

Chakri Day — April 6 is a national holiday to commemorate the founding of the Chakri dynasty.

Songkran — April 13 marks the Thai New Year. Essentially a religious holiday when lustral water is sprinkled on Buddha images, it has become, especially in Chiang Mai, a time of good-natured highjinks involving throwing water over one and all.

May

Ploughing Ceremony — Takes place at the Pramane Ground in Bangkok at the beginning of the planting season on a date determined by Brahman priests. Presided over by His Majesty the King, the ceremony involves the ritual ploughing by sacred oxen and the planting of specially blessed rice seeds. A prediction is made for the success of the year's harvest.

Labour Day — May 1 is an official Thai holiday.

Coronation Day — May 5 commemorates the coronation of the present King.

Visakha Bucha — The most important date in the Buddhist calendar celebrating the day (in different years) on which the Buddha was born, achieved enlightenment and died. It falls on the day of the full moon and there are candlelit processions around temples in the evening.

July

Asanha Bucha

Falling on the day of the full moon, this is the anniversary of the Buddha's first sermon to his first five disciples. It marks the beginning of Buddhist Lent, *Khao Phansa*, a three-month period of retreat for monks.

August

Queen's Birthday

August 12 is the celebration of Her Majesty Queen Sirikit's birthday. It is a public holiday and many buildings are decorated with coloured lights in honour of the occasion.

October

Ok Phansa

This holiday celebrates the Buddha's return to earth after spending one Lent season preaching in heaven. It also marks the end of the Lent period of retreat and the beginning of *Krathin*, the traditional time for presenting new robes and other gifts to monks at temples thoughout the country.

Chulalongkorn Day

October 23 is the anniversary of the death of King Chulalongkorn, Rama V. Floral tributes and incense are placed at the foot of the monarch's equestrian statue in front of the old National Assembly building.

November

Loy Krathong

Held on the night of the full moon, this enchanting festival pays homage to Mae Khongkha, goddess of rivers and waterways. Throughout the country Thais gather by rivers, canals, lakes and ponds to float *krathongs*, colourful little lotus-shaped "boats" bearing the traditional offerings of flowers, a candle, incense and a coin.

Golden Mount Fair

Bangkok's biggest temple fair held at Wat Saket by the Golden Mount.

Elephant Round-Up

An annual show in Surin featuring a large gathering of trained elephants which display work skills, perform games and parade in the battle regalia of old.

December

The King's Birthday

December 5 is the birthday of His Majesty King Bhumibol Adulyadej and is a public holiday. Public buildings are illuminated at night.

Constitution Day

December 10, a public holiday.

New Year's Eve

December 31, a public holiday.

Note: if any major event falls on the weekend, the next working day is taken as the public holiday.

A Great Parade

O ne of the most vivid memories of Ploi's childhood was the Tonsure Ceremony for Her Royal Highness the Princess Daughter.

For weeks before this was due to take place the whole Inner Court lived in a heightened state of pleasurable anticipation. News and rumours and speculations about the ceremonials and festivities to come were eagerly sought, passed on and commented upon from morning till night:—who had been selected to attend upon the Princess in the procession, what costume Her Royal Highness would be wearing for each of the three days while listening to the chanting of holy stanzas, how many kinds of entertainment, what presentations, performances and spectacles could be expected, and so on and so forth. Preparing for the event was half the fun. Everyone, it seemed, was either engaged in getting the Palace Fair ready or getting ready to go to the Palace Fair, or both. Old and young alike, the women of the Inner Court looked forward to putting on their best jewellery for the occasion; those who had pawned theirs were now trying to get them back at all costs, adding not a little to the general excitement by their frantic manoeuverings.

The first day of the event saw Choi and Ploi elbowing their way to the front line of the crowds waiting for the procession to pass on its way to the Outer Court of the Grand Palace. They waited for hours, drenched to the skin under the sweltering sun but with undampened high spirits. The conch shell trumpet finally sounded in the distance, telling them that His Majesty had seen the Princess Daughter into her gold palanquin and that they could now start craning their necks in earnest—and also standing firm on their appropriated bits of stone pavement against fellow parade-watchers, who were pressing and pushing on all sides. Choi was doing some pushing herself and yelling to Ploi that they mustn't lose each other. They were both laughing, and so were many people in the crowd.

The military band came first (no need to record that this was Ploi's first military band) playing a rousing march in the Farang style; then columns of marching soldiers, eyes gazing straight ahead, guns on erect shoulders, arms and legs moving in perfect unison. Choi and Ploi stared at them, then nodded at each other as if to say this was a good beginning, no doubt about it. The rat-a-tat-tat of the Farang drums fading away was succeeded by the ting-tang-ting of the Java drums, which emerged at the head of another group of musicians, whose ancient dress furnished a colourful contrast to the soldiers' uniform. The Java pipes filled the air with their heart-lifting notes as ranking officials and page-boys, their palms joined respectfully in a wai, walked slowly past the spectators. Next came the Victory Drum and Conch Trumpet Unit drumming and blowing in the midst of a waving white and gold forest of tiered umbrellas; sunshades and other lofty insignias of a Princess Royal. Mingled with the sound of the prepitious instruments was the crowd's murmuring noise, rising at times into words and phrases.

"Where's the palanquin? I can't see it."

"You will in a moment—can't you wait?"

"Ah—here come the brahmins!"

The white-robed brahmins came strewing grains of blessed rice along the path. Some of them fell where Ploi was standing and she picked them up, though only to lose them soon afterwards.

"Oh look at the handsome cuckoos!"

They were a pair of charmingly costumed little boys carrying feathers in their hands to represent a pair of Indian cuckoos. A few paces behind them strutted the "peacocks", who were followed in their turn by two pretty little girls holding gold and silver branches. Then a sigh, a heart-felt chorus of "How beautiful!" went up as, preceding the long train of attendants—courtiers, bearers, Pond Maidens, Fan Maidens, and a retinue of maids-in-waiting—Her Royal Highness appeared, seated in the Gold Vehicle, herself golden and sparkling from topknot to the tip of her toes. Some among the spectators had tears in their eyes, and a few old women were paying respects and sniffling happily at the same time. When the vehicle had passed, those in the crowd who had friends and relatives in the procession started to point them out to one another, beaming and talking more loudly than before.

Kukrit Pramoy, Si Phaendin
translated by Tulachandra

Recommended Reading

The best general history of Thailand is David Wyatt's **Thailand: A Short History** (New Haven, Yale University Press, 1984) which gives a good outline of the Bangkok period as well as all historical development prior to the founding of the present capital in 1782. For a brief historical sketch of the city through words and old photographs there is Steve Van Beek's **Bangkok Only Yesterday** (Hong King Publishing Co. Ltd., 1982) while the reigns of the present ruling Chakri dynasty are described in **Lords of Life** by Prince Chula Chakrabongse (Bangkok, DD Books, reprint 1982). **Old Bangkok** (Oxford University Press, 1986) by Michael Smithies offers a succinct outline of the city's early development.

There are attractive and profusely illustrated books on the city including volumes all simply titled **Bangkok** by John Blofeld and Philip Jones Griffiths (Time-Life Books, 1979); Ian Lloyd and William Warren (Times Editions, 1986); and Luca Invernizzi Tettoni and John Hoskin (also published by Times Editions, 1986.)

The most comprehensive country guidebook is **Guide to Thailand** by A. Clarac and M. Smithies (Kuala Lumpur, Oxford University Press/ DK Book House, 1981). This is the 'Baedeker' of Thailand with detailed descriptions of temples and historical monuments in Bangkok and throughout the country.

For a good survey of the country, its people, economy, administration, etc., there is the highly informative **Thailand in the 80s** published by the National Identity Board.

Among the various books on Thai classical art there are Jean Boisselier's two hefty tomes, **The Heritage of Thai Sculpture** (Weatherhill, 1974) and **Thai Painting** (Tokyo, Kodansha International, 1976), and M.C. Subhadradis Diskul's short but useful **Art in Thailand: A Brief History** (Bangkok, Silapakorn University, 1970). For a superbly illustrated general introduction to the subject there is **The Arts of Thailand** (Hong Kong, Travel Publishing Asia, 1985) written by Steve Van Beek and photographed by Luca Invernizzi Tettoni. Helen Bruce's **Nine Temples of Bangkok** (Bangkok, Chalermnit) gives interesting background information of the city's major Buddhist Temples.

Fascinating insights into Thai culture are given in Denis Segaller's **Thai Ways** (Bangkok, 1980) and **More Thai Ways** (Bangkok, 1982), while Carol Hollinger's **Mai Pen Rai** (Boston, Houghton Mifflin, 1965; reprinted by Weatherhill, 1977) is a humorous and most perceptive account of an expat's life in Bangkok in the late 1950s.

There are several interesting first-hand historical accounts which include descriptions of Bangkok and Thai life in the 19th century, notable among which are: **Temples and Elephants** (originally published in 1884 and now available in reprint editions by Oxford University Press and White Orchid Press, Bangkok) by Carl Bock;

The Kingdom and People of Siam by John Bowring (OUP/DK Book House, 1977 reprint of the 1857 first edition) and **A Week in Siam, January 1867** by the Marquis of Beauvoir (reprinted by the Siam Society, Bangkok, 1986). Also of note is Dr Malcolm Smith's **A Physician at the Court of Siam** (London 1947, now a OUP reprint), a revealing picture of the life of the royal household in the reign of King Rama V. Coming closer to the present day, Germaine Krull, who ran the Oriental Hotel in the years immediately following World War II, wrote an entertaining book of reminiscences called **Bangkok: Siam's City of Angels**. Jim Thompson, one time partner of Krull's and later silk tycoon, has become Bangkok's most famous expatriate with a fame enhanced by his still unexplained disappearance in Malaysia in 1967; his story is well told by William Warren in **Jim Thompson: The Legendary American of Thailand** (Houghton Mifflin, 1970).

Basic Thai Vocabulary

Thai, like Chinese and various other more or less related languages and dialects in East and Southeast Asia, is a tonal, mostly monosyllabic language: that is, each spoken syllable can function on its own as a word, and has a certain pitch or intonation assigned to it which is as important in identifying it and distinguishing it from other words as the consonant and vowel sounds it is otherwise composed of. This aspect of the language makes it particularly difficult for speakers of non-tonal languages (including speakers of European languages) to learn. Complicating the picture even further is the Thai alphabet, based on (but yet different from) an ancient south Indian script. And there is no standard romanization system, resulting in a variety of spellings for even common place names: Ayutthaya/Ayudhaya, Chiang Mai/Chieng-mai, Chao Phraya/Chao Phya, etc.

Below is a short list of the words and phrases most easily and usefully learned by the short-term visitor. Even the most mangled attempt to speak Thai is welcomed with friendly laughter and encouragement, and is a good way to break the ice (and often bring down prices in shops and markets). For those who envision a more serious committment to learning Thai, dictionaries and phrase books are widely available; the truly devoted should contact the American University Alumni Association (A.U.A.), which runs a number of Thai and English language programs throughout the country. (A.U.A., 179 Rajdamri Road, Bangkok; tel. 252-7069.)

Numbers

one	neung	หนึ่ง
two	sorng	สอง
three	sam	สาม
four	see	สี่
five	haa	ห้า
six	hok	หก
seven	jet	เจ็ด.
eight	paet	แปด
nine	kao	เก้า
ten	sip	สิบ
eleven	sip-et	สิบเอ็ด
twelve	sip sorng	สิบสอง
fifteen	sip haa	สิบห้า
twenty	yee sip	ยี่สิบ
twenty-one	yee sip-et	ยี่สิบเอ็ด
twenty-two	yee sip sorng	ยี่สิบสอง
thirty	sam sip	สามสิบ
fifty	haa sip	ห้าสิบ
one hundred	neung roi	หนึ่งร้อย
one thousand	neung paen	หนึ่งพัน
ten thousand	neung meun	หนึ่งหมื่น
one hundred thousand	neung saen	หนึ่งแสน
one million	neung laan	หนึ่งล้าน

Basic Phrases

thank you	khawp khun khrap (male)	ขอบคุณครับ
	khawp khun khaa (female)	ขอบคุณค่ะ
hello, goodbye	sawat dee (khrap or khaa)	สวัสดีค่ะ หรือ ครับ
excuse me	khor thot .	ขอโทษ
never mind	mai pen rai	ไม่เป็นไร
no	mai	ไม่
yes	chai (it is) or simply	ใช่, ครับ หรือ ค่ะ
	"khrap" or "kha"	
how are you?	sabai dee reu?	สบายดีเหรอ
I'm fine	sabai dee (khrap . .)	สบายดี (ครับ หรือ ค่ะ)
I don't feel well	mai sabai (khrap . .)	ไม่สบาย

Questions and directions

what is your name?	khun cheu arai khrap?	คุณชื่ออะไรครับ
my name is . . .	phom (male) chun	ผมชื่อ (ผู้ชาย), ฉันชื่อ (ผู้หญิง)
	(female) cheu . . .	
where is . . .	you nai?	อยู่ไหน
I want to go to . . .	yaak ja pai . . .	อยากจะไป
turn left	leou sai	เลี้ยวซ้าย
turn right	leou khwa	เลี้ยวขวา
straight ahead	trong pai	ตรงไป
stop here	yoot tee nee	หยุดที่นี่
how much does this cost?	nee baht taw rai?	นี่บาทเท่าไหร่

Places

hotel	rawng ram	โรงแรม
street	tanon	ถนน
side street	soi	ซอย
bus station	sat-hani rot meh	สถานีรถเมล์
railway station	sat-hani rot fai	สถานีรถไฟ
airport	sanam bin	สนามบิน
	(in Bangkok	(ในกรุงเทพ เรียก
	'Don Muang')	"ดอนเมือง")
city	nakhon	นคร
town	muang	เมือง
village	ban	บ้าน
beach	haat	หาด
island	koh	เกาะ
mountain, hill	doi, khao	เขา, ดอย
restaurant	raan ahaan	ร้านอาหาร
hospital	rong phaya-bahn	โรงพยาบาล
post office	prai-sannee	ไปรษณีย์
police station	sat-hani tamruat	สถานีตำรวจ
embassy	sat-han toot	สถานทูต
bathroom	hawng nam	ห้องน้ำ

room	hawng	ห้อง
market	talatt	ตลาด
river	menam	แม่น้ำ
nation	prahtett	ประเทศ

Useful words

today	wan nee	วันนี้
yesterday	meua wan nee	เมื่อวานนี้
tomorrow	proong nee	พรุ่งนี้
day	wan	วัน
week	ahtit	อาทิตย์
month	deun	เดือน
year	pee	ปี
hungry	hew kao	หิวข้าว
thirsty	hew nam	หิวน้ำ
food	ahahn	อาหาร
water	nam	น้ำ
train	rot fai	รถไฟ
auto	rot yon	รถยนต์
boat	reua	เรือ
airplane	kreung bin	เครื่องบิน
taxi	taksee	แท็กซี่

Food

water	nam	น้ำ
salt	kreua	เกลือ
sugar, sweet	wan	น้ำตาล, หวาน
chilli pepper	plik	พริก
beef	neua	เนื้อ
pork	moo	หมู
chicken	gai	ไก่
eggs	kai	ไข่
fish	plaa	ปลา
vegetables	pahk	ผัก
fruit	pohlamai	ผลไม้
rice	khao	ข้าว
to eat	khao	ทานข้าว
to drink	deum	ดื่ม
soup	tom	ต้ม
coffee	cafe	กาแฟ
tea	cha	ชา

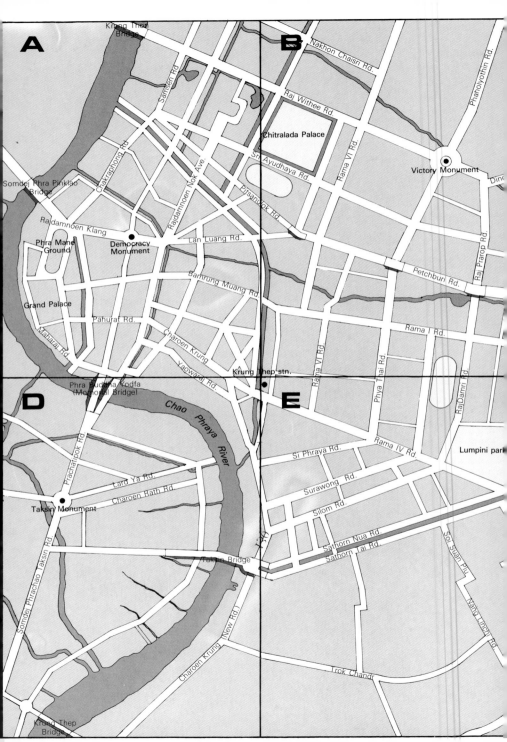

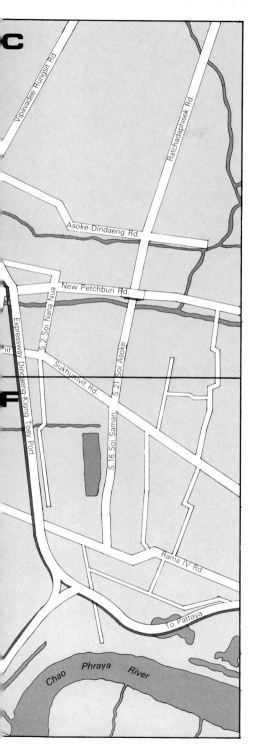

BANGKOK MASTER MAP

In defiance of the official Thai-English language transcription system, many Thai place names, especially streets, are spelled in endlessly different ways. In some cases a single street may have six different English spellings, all vaguely similar. For instance Raja-damnoen Rd., Ratchadamnoen Rd., Raj Damnern Rd., Rajdamnoen Rd., Raj Damnoen Rd. and Rachdam-noen Rd. appear on various maps. The publishers, therefore, have given up trying to make the street spellings consistent, and the tourist must be prepared to 'interpret' various spellings since that is the reality they face while exploring the city.

LEGEND

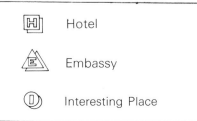

Ⓗ	Hotel
Ⓔ	Embassy
Ⓘ	Interesting Place

A

Krungthon Bridge

Sukhothai Rd.

Rajsima Nua Rd.

Pichai Rd

Raj Withee

Chao Phraya River

Samsen Rd.

Rajsima Tai Rd.

Parliament

Dusi

Throne Hall

Sri Ayudhaya Rd.

Wat Benchama Borphit

Trok Wat Sam Phya

Visut Kasat Rd.

Krung Kasem Rd.

Pitsanulo

Amarin Rd.

Somdej Phra Pinklao Bridge

Pra Arthit Rd.

Chakraphong Rd.

Phra Sumeru Rd.

Prachathipatai Rd.

Thai

Rajdamnoen Nok Ave.

Boxing Stadium

Luk Laung

Krung Kasem R

National Theatre

Rajdamnoen Klang Ave.

National Museum

Royal

Democracy Monument

Lan Laung Rd.

Phra Chan Rd.

Asdang Rd.

Tanao Rd.

Dinso Rd.

Bamrung Muang Rd.

Phra Mane Ground

Golden Mountain

Bamrung Mung Rd.

Wat Phra Keo

Sananchai Rd.

Unakan Rd.

Mahachai Rd.

Worajak Rd.

Sau Pa Rd.

Phlapplachai Rd.

Maharaj Rd.

Grand Palace

Laung Rd.

Charaen Krung (New Rd.)

Wat Po

Pahurat Rd.

Mitrichit Rd.

Mitrphan

Wat Arun

Ban Moh Rd.

Tri Petch Rd.

Jakrawad Rd.

Rajwongs Rd.

Yaowarai Rd.

Santiparp Rd.

Vang Daem Rd.

Krung Kasem

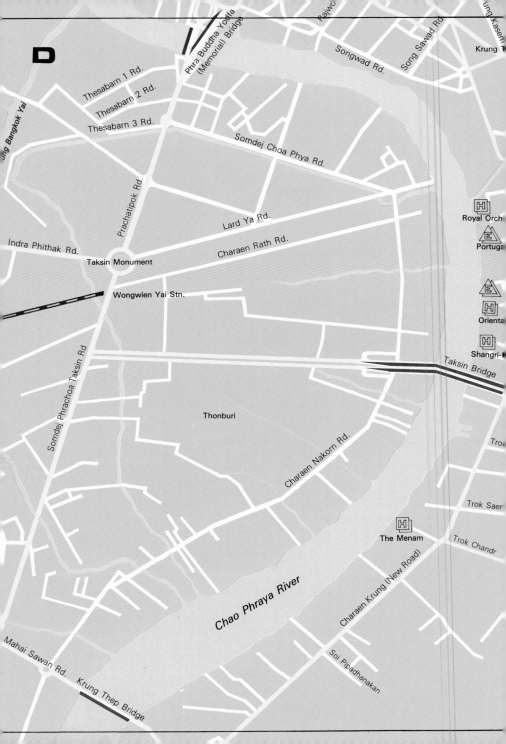

C

Soi Sailom 2.

Vipavadee Rangsit Rd.

Pracha Songkhro Rd.

Soi Promphan

China

Ratchadaphisek Rd.

Expressway

Asoke Dindaeng Rd.

Klong Samsen

T.V. Channel 9

Makasan Stn.

gkok Palace

Eastern Railway Line.

New Petchburi Rd.

Klong Saensaep

Siam Hotel

Japan

Hilton.

Brazil

Swiss

itish

Pakistan

Ploenchit Rd.

Soi Ruenrudi

Soi Nana Nua

Soi Lertsin 1

S. 5 Soi Lertsin 2

S. 7 Soi Ruan Chit.

S. 9 Soi Chaiyos

S. 11 Soi Sangchan

S. 13 Soi Rumjai

S. 15 Soi Wadhana

S. 19 Soi Asoke

S. 21 Soi Prasanmitr

S. 23 Soi Daeng Prasert

S. 25 Soi Raj Montri

Soi Akphat

Soi Prachan Khadi

New Imperial

Sri Lanka

Ambassador

Nana

Manhattan

India

Chaovalit

Sukhumvit

S. 2 Soi Phasuk

Soi Sawasdi

am.

Index to Place Names